The Postmodern Condition

MANCHESTER
1824

Manchester University Press

The Postmodern Condition:
A Report on Knowledge

Jean-François Lyotard

Translation from the French by
Geoff Bennington and Brian Massumi
Foreword by Fredric Jameson

Manchester University Press

Published in the United Kingdom by Manchester University Press, Oxford Road, Manchester M13 9NR

First impression 1984, first reprinted 1986

British Library Cataloguing in Publication Data is available

ISBN 978 0 7190 1450 5 paperback

"Answering the Question: What is Postmodernism?" appears in this book courtesy of the University of Wisconsin Press (English translation of this essay by Regis Durand copyright © 1983 by University of Wisconsin Press; the essay appears in Ihab Hassan and Sally Hassan, eds, *Innovation/Renovation* [Madison: University of Wisconsin Press, 1983] and courtesy of Jean Piel, editor of *Critique*, where the essay originally appeared as "Response a la question: qu'est-ce que le postmoderne?" in *Critique*, number 419 (April 1982).

Printed by the MPG Books Group in the UK

Contents

Foreword
Fredric Jameson

This seemingly neutral review of a vast body of material on contemporary science and problems of knowledge or information proves
on closer inspection to be a kind of crossroads in which a number of
different themes—a number of different books—intersect and
problematize each other. For Jean-François Lyotard's discussion of
the consequences of the new views of scientific research and its
paradigms, opened up by theorists like Thomas Kuhn and Paul
Feyerabend, is also a thinly yeiled polemic against Jürgen Habermas's
concept of a "legitimation crisis" and vision of a "noisefree," transparent, fully communicational society. Meanwhile the title of the
book, with its fashionable theme of postmodernism provocatively in
evidence, opens up this subject matter, at least by implication, in
the directions of aesthetics and economics, since postmodernism as
it is generally understood involves a radical break, both with a dominant culture and aesthetic, and with a rather different moment of
socioeconomic organization against which its structural novelties
and innovations are measured: a new social and economic moment
(or even system), which has variously been called media society, the
"society of the spectacle" (Guy Debord), consumer society (or the
"société de consommation"), the "bureaucratic society of controlled
consumption" (Henri Lefebvre), or "postindustrial society" (Daniel
Bell). It may also be assumed that this ostensibly technical and

impersonal handbook is also a significant move in the development
of Lyotard's own philosophical views, whose combative and prophetic
voice, familiar to the readers of his other works, will surprise by its
relative silence here. Finally, and closely related to this last, *The
Postmodern Condition* presents us with significant methodological
operations, which, although they draw on a whole very rich contemporary tradition of narrative analysis nonetheless strike a relatively
isolated and unusual note in the whole range of contemporary philosophical research.

Lyotard's official subject matter—the status of science and technology, of technocracy and the control of knowledge and information
today—is perhaps the most familiar material for the American reader,
yet it opens immediately and instructively onto all the other themes
I have just enumerated. "Doing science," for instance, involves its
own kind of legitimation (why is it that our students do not do laboratory work in alchemy? why is Immanuel Velikovsky considered to
be an eccentric?) and may therefore be investigated as a subset of
the vaster political problem of the legitimation of a whole social
order (a theme, which, formulated in that particular code or terminology, is associated with the work of Habermas). Doing "normal"
science and participating in lawful and orderly social reproduction
are then two phenomena—better still, two *mysteries*—that ought to
be able to illuminate one another.

But as the term *crisis* in Habermas's title, as well as the prefix
post in that of Lyotard, reminds us, legitimation becomes visible as
a problem and an object of study only at the point in which it is
called into question. As far as science is concerned, this crisis may be
taken to be that of which the historical theories of Kuhn or Feyerabend stand as crucial symptoms: it would seem rather less important
to decide whether those theories imply that we are now in a position
to think or conceptualize scientific research in a very different way
from the Newtonian period, or on the contrary that we now actually
do science in a different way. At any rate, this "break" now links up
with the other thematics of Lyotard's essay by way of an event
generally taken primarily to be an aesthetic one, although it has
relatively immediate philosophical and ideological analogues: I am
referring to the so-called crisis of representation, in which an essentially realistic epistemology, which conceives of representation as the
reproduction, for subjectivity, of an objectivity that lies outside it—
projects a mirror theory of knowledge and art, whose fundamental
evaluative categories are those of adequacy, accuracy, and Truth
itself. It is in terms of this crisis that the transition, in the history of

form, from a novelistic "realism" of the Lukácsean variety to the various now classical "high" modernisms, has been described: the cognitive vocation of science would however seem even more disastrously impaired by the analogous shift from a representational to a nonrepresentational practice. Lyotard here ingeniously "saves" the coherence of scientific research and experiment by recasting its now seemingly non- or postreferential "epistemology" in terms of linguistics, and in particular of theories of the performative (J. L. Austin), for which the justification of scientific work is not to produce an adequate model or replication of some outside reality, but rather simply to produce *more* work, to generate new and fresh scientific *énoncés* or statements, to make you have "new ideas" (P. B. Medawar), or, best of all (and returning to the more familiar aesthetics of high modernism), again and again to "make it new": "Au fond de l'Inconnu pour trouver du *nouveau!*"

However this novel way of relegitimizing contemporary science is understood or evaluated—and it has many family resemblances elsewhere in contemporary thought[1] —it then retrospectively allows Lyotard to sketch a narrative analysis of the older forms of scientific legitimation, whose collapse in our own time imposes such desperate solutions, such remarkable last-minute salvage operations.

The two great legitimizing "myths" or narrative archetypes (*récits*) are also something of a complication, in that they reproduce the denotative argument of the book in a connotative or autoreferent spiral. For the two great myths disengaged by Lyotard and identified as the alternate justifications for institutional scientific research up to our own period—that of the liberation of humanity and that of the speculative unity of all knowledge (qua philosophical system)— are also national myths and reproduce the very polemic in which Lyotard's own book wishes to intervene. The first —political, militant, activist—is of course the tradition of the French eighteenth century and the French Revolution, a tradition for which philosophy is already politics and in which Lyotard must himself clearly be ranged. The second is of course the Germanic and Hegelian tradition —a contemplative one, organized around the value of totality rather than that of commitment, and a tradition to which Lyotard's philosophical adversary, Habermas, still—however distantly—remains affiliated. The conflict can be dramatized and magnified if for these names we substitute even more prestigious ones whose philosophical differences are even more sharply articulated: compare, for example, Gilles Deleuze's influential celebration of schizophrenia (in books like the *Anti-Oedipus*) with T. W. Adorno's no less influential and characteristic denunciations of cultural reification and fetishization. The opposition can also be rotated in a psychoanalytical direction, in which case a characteristically French affirmation of the "decentered subject" or the illusion of the coherent self or ego is set off against more traditional Frankfurt School defenses of psychic "autonomy."

Still, these traditions are not altogether so continuous or symmetrical as I have just suggested. Lyotard is, after all, writing in the wake of a certain French "post-Marxism," that is, an enormous reaction on all levels against various Marxist and Communist traditions in France, whose prime target on the philosophical level is the Hegel/Lukács concept of "totality" (often overhastily assimilated to Stalinism or even to the Leninist party on the political level). Lyotard's own philosophical break with Marxism (he was a member of the important *Socialisme ou barbarie* group in the 1950s and early 1960s)[2] largely antedates this more recent, rather McCarthyist moment in France (itself since overtaken by the unexpected Socialist landslide of 1981); but it clearly makes for a situation in which Habermas can still stand in for the totalizing and dialectical German tradition, while Lyotard's own philosophical relationship to the politicized French one has become far more problematic and complex. Indeed, I want to show a little later on that one significant "libidinal" subtext of the present volume consists of a symbolic effort to clarify this tangled plot as well. At any rate, Habermas's vision of an evolutionary social leap into a new type of rational society, defined in communicational terms as "the communication community of those affected, who as participants in a practical discourse test the validity claims of norms and, to the extent that they accept them with reasons, arrive at the conviction that in the given circumstances the proposed norms are 'right,' "[3] is here explicitly rejected by Lyotard as the unacceptable remnant of a "totalizing" philosophical tradition and as the valorization of conformist, when not "terrorist," ideals of consensus. (Indeed, insofar as Habermas will invoke a liberatory rhetoric as well, there is a sense in which, for Lyotard, this philosophical position unites everything that is unacceptable about *both* traditions and myths of legitimation.)

Before examining the position in terms of which such critiques are made, however, we must turn at least parenthetically to the methodological perspective developed here, in which legitimation is secured in terms of master-narratives of the two types already described. The admission to France of such Anglo-American linguistic notions as that of Austin's "performative" is now largely an accomplished fact (although a rather unexpected development). In a more general way, the linguistic dimensions of what used to be called French structuralism and the seemingly more static possibilities of a dominant semiotics have in recent years been corrected and augmented by a return to pragmatics, to the analysis of language situations and games, and of language itself as an unstable exchange between its speakers, whose utterances are now seen less as a process of the transmission of information or messages, or in terms of some network of signs or even signifying systems, than as (to use one of Lyotard's favorite figures) the "taking of tricks," the trumping of a communicational adversary, an essentially conflictual relationship between tricksters— and not as a well-regulated and noisefree "passing of tokens from hand to hand" (Mallarmé on denotative speech). We have already observed Lyotard's promotion of the "performative" to the very fundamental principle of contemporary science itself; what is even more striking in his methodological perspective, however—indeed, to my knowledge he is one of the few professional philosophers of stature anywhere *formally* to have (although Paul Ricoeur and Alistair McIntyre also come to mind) drawn this momentous conse- quence—is the way in which narrative is affirmed, not merely as a significant new field of research, but well beyond that as a central instance of the human mind and a mode of thinking fully as legiti- mate as that of abstract logic.

A lengthy methodological parenthesis defends this proposition, which at once itself becomes a kind of historical narrative in its own right, since—particularly in the context of a discussion of *science*— it is obvious that one of the features that characterizes more "scien- tific" periods of history, and most notably capitalism itself, is the relative retreat of the claims of narrative or storytelling knowledge in the face of those of the abstract, denotative, or logical and cognitive procedures generally associated with science or positivism. This parenthesis once again complicates the arguments of *The Postmodern Condition* insofar as it becomes itself a symptom of the state it seeks to diagnose—its own return to narrative arguments being fully as revealing an example of the legitimation crisis of the older cognitive and epistemological scientific world-view as any of the other develop- ments enumerated in the text. Lyotard does indeed characterize one recent innovation in the analysis of science as a view of scientific experiments as so many smaller narratives or stories to be worked out. On the other hand, paradoxically, this revival of an essentially narrative view of "truth," and the vitality of small narrative units at work everywhere *locally* in the present social system, are accom- panied by something like a more global or totalizing "crisis" in the narrative function in general, since, as we have seen, the older master- narratives of legitimation no longer function in the service of scientific research—nor, by implication, anywhere else (e.g., we no longer believe in political or historical teleologies, or in the great "actors" and "subjects" of history—the nation-state, the proletariat, the party, the West, etc.). This seeming contradiction can be resolved, I believe, by taking a further step that Lyotard seems unwilling to do in the present text, namely to posit, not the disappearance of the great master-narratives, but their passage underground as it were, their continuing but now *unconscious* effectivity as a way of "thinking about" and acting in our current situation. This persistence of buried master-narratives in what I have elsewhere called our "political unconscious," I will try shortly to demonstrate on the occasion of the present text as well.

What is most striking in Lyotard's differentiation between storytelling and "scientific" abstraction is its unexpected modulation towards a Nietzschean thematics of history. In effect, indeed, for Lyotard the fundamental distinction between these two forms of knowledge lies in their relationship to temporality, and in particular in their relationship to the retention of the past. Narrative, whose formal properties become magnified in prosody and in the rhythmic features of traditional tales, proverbs, and the like, is here characterized as a way of *consuming* the past, a way of forgetting: "as meter takes precedence over accent in the production of sound (spoken or not), time ceases to be a support for memory to become an immemorial beating that, in the absence of a noticeable separation between periods, prevents their being numbered and consigns them to oblivion" (section 6). One recalls the great and still influential essay of Nietzsche on the debilitating influence of historiography and of the fidelity to the past and the dead that an obsession with history seems to encourage. The Nietzschean "strength to *forget* the past"—in preparation for the mutation of the superman to come—is here paradoxically redeployed as a property of storytelling itself, of precisely those narratives, heroic or other, in which we have been taught to see a form of primitive data storage or of social reproduction. What this formulation does very sharply achieve, at any rate, is the radical differentiation between the consumption of the past in narrative and its storage, hoarding, and capitalization in "science" and scientific thought: a mode of understanding that, like the first surplus on the economic level, will little by little determine a whole range of ever more complex and extensive institutional objectifications—first in writing; then in libraries, universities, museums; with the breakthrough in our own period to microstorage, computerized data, and data banks of hitherto unimaginable proportions, whose control or even ownership is, as Herbert Schiller and others have warned us (and as Lyotard is very well aware), one of the crucial *political* issues of our own time.

We thus return to the thematics of science and knowledge in its social form: one that raises issues of social class—is the technocracy produced by such a primacy of knowledge a bureaucracy or a whole new class?—and of socioeconomic analysis—is this moment of advanced industrial society a structural variant of classical capitalism or a mutation and the dawning of a wholly new social structure in which, as Daniel Bell and other theoreticians of the concept of a properly "postindustrial society" have argued, it is now science, knowledge, technological research, rather than industrial production and the extraction of surplus value, that is the "ultimately determining instance"?

In reality, two distinct and overlapping questions are raised simultaneously by these two interrelated theoretical problems, which to his credit Lyotard does not seek here in peremptory fashion to resolve. The problem is finally that of the nature of a mode of production, and in particular the nature of the capitalist mode of production and the structural variations of which it is capable. The question may therefore be rephrased as a question about Marxism: do the categories developed there for the analysis of classical capitalism still retain their validity and their explanatory power when we turn to the multinational and media societies of today with their "third-stage" technologies? The persistence of issues of power and control, particularly in the increasing monopolization of information by private business, would seem to make an affirmative answer unavoidable, and to reconfirm the privileged status of Marxism as a mode of analysis of capitalism proper.

But the question has often been taken to involve a second set of answers or consequences as well, having to do with the end of capitalism, the possibility of revolution, and, first and foremost, the continuing function of the industrial working class as the fundamental revolutionary "subject of history." It has at least historically been possible for intellectuals and militants to recognize the explanatory power of Marxism as the privileged mode of analysis of capitalism (including the particular social moment that is our own society) and, at one and the same time, to abandon the traditional Marxian vision of revolution and socialism, mainly out of a conviction that the industrial working class (in any case defined by its relationship to productive technologies of the first and second type, rather than the third, cybernetic or nuclear variety) no longer occupies the strategic position of power in this social formation. A stronger theoretical form of this proposition would then be derivable in the notion that social classes—of the classical type defined by Marxism—no longer function as such today, but are rather displaced by different, non-class formations such as bureaucracy and technocracy (and this would seem to be the position of Lyotard, whose formative political work in the *Socialisme ou barbarie* group turned precisely around the analysis of bureaucracy in the Eastern countries).

The question of social class, and in particular of the "proletariat" and its existence, is hopelessly confused when such arguments conflate the problem of a theoretical category of analysis (social class) with the empirical question about the mood or influence of workers in this or that society today (they are no longer revolutionary, bourgeoisified, etc.). More orthodox Marxists will agree with the most radical post⁻ or anti-Marxist positions in at least this, that Marxism as a coherent philosophy (or better still, a "unity of theory and praxis") stands or falls with the matter of social class.

What one can at least suggest here is that with Ernest Mandel's theorization of a third stage of capitalism beyond that of the classical or market capitalism analyzed in *Capital* itself, and that of the monopoly stage or stage of "imperialism" proposed by Lenin, there exists a properly Marxian alternative to non- or anti-Marxist theories of "consumer" or "postindustrial" society today, theories of which Daniel Bell's is no doubt the most influential. Mandel indeed undertakes to show that all of the features mobilized by Bell to document the end of capitalism as such—in particular the new primacy of science and technological invention, and of the technocracy generated by that privileged position, as well as the shift from the older industrial technologies to the newer informational ones—can be accounted for in classical Marxist terms, as indices of a new and powerful, original, global expansion of capitalism, which now specifically penetrates the hitherto precapitalist enclaves of Third World agriculture and of First World culture, in which, in other words, capital more definitively secures the colonization of Nature and the Unconscious: "This new period [1940 to 1965] was characterized, among other things, by the fact that alongside machine-made industrial consumer goods (as from the early 19th century) and machine-made machines (as from the mid-19th century), we now find machine-produced raw materials and foodstuffs. Late capitalism, far from representing a 'post-industrial society,' thus appears as the period in which all branches of the economy are fully industrialized for the first time; to which one could further add the increasing mechanization of the sphere of circulation (with the exception of pure repair services) and the increasing mechanization of the super-structure."[4]

This description is also quite consistent with the Frankfurt School's conception of the "culture industry" and the penetration of commodity fetishism into those realms of the imagination and the psyche which had, since classical German philosophy, always been taken as some last impregnable stronghold against the instrumental logic of capital. What remains problematical about such conceptions—and about mediatory formulations such as that of Guy Debord, for whom "the image is the last stage of commodity reification"—is of course the difficulty of articulating cultural and informational commodities with the labor theory of value, the methodological problem of reconciling an analysis in terms of quantity and in particular of labor time (or of the sale of labor power in so many units) with the nature of "mental" work and of nonphysical and nonmeasurable "commodities" of the type of informational bits or indeed of media or entertainment "products." On the other hand, the posing of the category of "mode of production" as the fundamental one of Marxian social analysis and the endorsement of a "problematic" that asks such systemic questions about contemporary society would seem to remain essential for political people who are still committed to radical social change and transformation. Indeed, it is precisely as a contribution to this general problematic that Lyotard's little book is valuable, even though, as we shall see shortly, its author by no means counts himself among revolutionaries of the traditional kind.

If the changing status of science and knowledge (and of its experts) leads us to the question about the nature of this mode of production as a system and a functional whole, this second, larger issue returns us, after a considerable detour, to the problem of culture, and in particular of the existence or not of some properly "postmodernist" culture. For although the category of the mode of production has sometimes been misunderstood as a narrowly economic or "productionist" one, its adequate solution clearly demands a structural examination and positioning of the superstructural levels of a given social formation and, most urgently, the function and space to be assigned to culture itself: no satisfactory model of a given mode of production can exist without a theory of the historically and dialectically specific and unique role of "culture" within it.

Here Lyotard's sketch is tantalizing and finally frustrating; for the formal limitation of his essay to the problem of "knowledge" has tended to exclude an area—culture—that has been of the greatest importance to him in his other writings, as he has been one of the most keenly committed of contemporary thinkers anywhere to the whole range and variety of avant-garde and experimental art today. This very commitment to the experimental and the new, however, determine an aesthetic that is far more closely related to the traditional ideologies of high modernism proper than to current postmodernisms, and is indeed—paradoxically enough—very closely related to the conception of the revolutionary nature of high modernism that Habermas faithfully inherited from the Frankfurt School.

Thus, although he has polemically endorsed the slogan of a "postmodernism" and has been involved in the defense of some of its more controversial productions, Lyotard is in reality quite unwilling to posit a postmodernist stage radically different from the period of high modernism and involving a fundamental historical and cultural break with this last.[5] Rather, seeing postmodernism as a discontent with an disintegration of this or that high modernist style—a moment in the perpetual "revolution" and innovation of high modernism, to be succeeded by a fresh burst of formal invention—in a striking formula he has characterized postmodernism, not as that which follows modernism and its particular legitimation crisis, but rather as a cyclical moment that returns before the emergence of ever *new* modernisms in the stricter sense.

There is then here reproduced something of the celebration of modernism as its first ideologues projected it—a constant and ever more dynamic revolution in the languages, forms, and tastes of art (not yet assimilated to the commercial revolutions in fashion and commodity styling we have since come to grasp as an immanent rhythm of capitalism itself); to which a later wave of more explicitly left-wing and often Marxist ideologues and aesthetes after World War II will add an explicit *political* dimension—so that the revolutionary aesthetic of the modern will sometimes be grasped by the Frankfurt School, but also by the Tel Quel and Screen groups, in the more literal sense of critical negation when not of outright social and psychological transformation. Lyotard's own aesthetic retains much of this protopolitical thrust; his commitment to cultural and formal innovation still valorizes culture and its powers in much the same spirit in which the Western avant-garde has done so since the fin de siècle.

On the other hand, it would seem that the assimilation of postmodernism to this older conception of high modernism and its negative, critical, or revolutionary vocation deproblematizes a far more interesting and complex situation, which is part of the dilemma posed by "late capitalism" (or consumer or postindustrial society, etc.) in those other areas of science and technology, production, social change, and the like. Here it seems to me that Habermas—working to be sure within the far more suffocating and McCarthyist atmosphere of the Federal Republic—has a much keener sense of the political stakes involved in this seemingly theoretical matter than Lyotard has been willing to allow for. For Habermas, indeed, post-modernism involves the explicit repudiation of the modernist tradi-tion—the return of the middle-class philistine or *Spiessbuerger* rejec-tion of modernist forms and values—and as such the expression of a new social conservatism.[6]

His diagnosis is confirmed by that area in which the question of postmodernism has been mostly acutely posed, namely in architec-ture,[7] whose great high modernists, the architects of the International Style—Le Corbusier, Frank Lloyd Wright—were very precisely revolutionaries in the senses enumerated above: proponents of innovations in form and transformations in architectural space that could be expected in and of themselves to transform social life as a whole and, by replacing political revolution (as Le Corbusier put it), to serve as the latter's substitute (but in that form, the idea is as old as Schiller's *Aesthetic Education of Humankind*). Postmodernism certainly means a return of all the old antimodernist prejudices (as in Tom Wolfe's recent *From the Bauhaus to Our House*), but it was also, objectively, the recognition of a basic failure on the architects' own terms: the new buildings of Le Corbusier and Wright did not finally change the world, nor even modify the junk space of late capitalism, while the Mallarmean "zero degree" of Mies's towers quite unexpectedly began to generate a whole overpopulation of the shoddiest glass boxes in all the major urban centers in the world. This is the sense in which high modernism can be definitively certi-fied as dead and as a thing of the past: its Utopian ambitions were unrealizable and its formal innovations exhausted.

This is however not at all the conclusion that Habermas and Lyo-tard draw from what they think of in their different ways as the postmodernist movement: for both of them a return to the older critical high modernism is still possible, just as (equally anachronis-tically) for Lukács, writing in the thick of the high modernist period, a return to some older premodernist realism was still possible. Yet if one is willing—as both Habermas and Lyotard are—to posit the emergence of some new state of social relations (even leaving aside the question of whether this is to be considered a whole new mode of production in its own right or not), then it does not seem particularly daring to posit some equivalent modification in the very role and dynamic of cultural production itself, something indeed one ought to be able to entertain dialectically, without any needless moralizing. Postmodernist architecture, for example, comes before us as a peculiar analogue to neoclassicism, a play of ("historicist") allusion and quotation that has renounced the older high modernist rigor and that itself seems to recapitulate a whole range of traditional Western aesthetic strategies: we therefore have a mannerist postmodernism (Michael Graves), a baroque postmodernism (the Japanese), a rococo postmodernism (Charles Moore), a neoclassicist postmodernism (the French, particularly Christian de Portzamparc), and probably even a "high modernist" postmodernism in which modernism is itself the object of the postmodernist pastiche. This is a rich and creative movement, of the greatest aesthetic play and delight, that can perhaps be most rapidly characterized as a whole by two important features: first, the falling away of the protopolitical vocation and the terrorist stance of the older modernism and, second, the eclipse of all of the affect (depth, anxiety, terror, the emotions of the monumental) that marked high modernism and its replacement by what Coleridge would have called fancy or Schiller aesthetic play, a commitment to surface and to the *superficial* in all the senses of the word.

It was, however, precisely to the superficial (in all those senses) that a certain French poststructuralism invited us, not excluding the earlier works of Lyotard himself: this is, however, the moment in which aesthetics gives way to ethics, in which the problem of the postmodern (even in its relationship to new forms of science and knowledge) becomes that of one's more fundamental attitude toward the new social formation—the moment, finally, in which what I have called the deeper repressed or buried symbolic narrative of *The Postmodern Condition* comes at length into view.

Lyotard's affiliations here would seem to be with the *Anti-Oedipus* of Gilles Deleuze and Félix Guattari, who also warned us, at the end of that work, that the schizophrenic ethic they proposed was not at all a revolutionary one, but a way of surviving under capitalism, producing fresh desires within the structural limits of the capitalist mode of production as such.[8] Lyotard's celebration of a related ethic emerges most dramatically in the context of that repudiation of Habermas's consensus community already mentioned, in which the dissolution of the self into a host of networks and relations, of contradictory codes and interfering messages, is prophetically valorized (section 4). This view not surprisingly will then determine Lyotard's ultimate vision of science and knowledge today as a search, not for consensus, but very precisely for "instabilities," as a practice of *paralogism*, in which the point is not to reach agreement but to undermine from within the very framework in which the previous "normal science" had been conducted. The rhetoric in which all this is conveyed is to be sure one of struggle, conflict, the agonic in a quasi-heroic sense; nor must we forget Lyotard's related vision of nonhegemonic Greek philosophy (the Stoics, the Cynics, the Sophists), as the guerrilla war of the marginals, the foreigners, the non-Greeks, against the massive and repressive Order of Aristotle and his successors.[9] On the other hand, aesthetics sometimes functions as an unpleasant mirror; and we need perhaps at least momentarily to reflect on the peculiar consonance between Lyotard's scientific "free play" and the way in which postmodernist architecture has taught us to "learn from Las Vegas" (Robert Venturi) and "to make ourselves at home in our alienated being" (Marx on Hegel's conception of Absolute Spirit). This is, at any rate, the deepest, most contradictory, but also the most urgent level of Lyotard's book: that of a narrative which—like all narrative—must generate the illusion of "an imaginary resolution of real contradictions" (Lévi-Strauss).

The formal problem involved might be expressed this way: how to do without narrative by means of narrative itself? On the political and social level, indeed, narrative in some sense always meant the negation of capitalism: on the one hand, for instance, narrative knowledge is here opposed to "scientific" or abstract knowledge as precapitalism to capitalism proper. Yet—as became clear when the narrative legitimations of science itself were evoked at their moment of crisis and dissolution—narrative also means something like *teleology*. The great master-narratives here are those that suggest that something beyond capitalism is possible, something radically different; and they also "legitimate" the praxis whereby political militants seek to bring that radically different future social order into being. Yet both master-narratives of science have become peculiarly repugnant or embarrassing to First World intellectuals today: the rhetoric of liberation has for example been denounced with passionate ambivalence by Michel Foucault in the first volume of his *History of Sexuality*; while the rhetoric of totality and totalization that derived from what I have called the Germanic or Hegelian tradition is the object of a kind of instinctive or automatic denunciation by just about everybody.

Lyotard's insistence on *narrative analysis* in a situation in which the narratives themselves henceforth seem impossible is his declaration of intent to remain political and contestatory; that is, to avoid one possible and even logical resolution to the dilemma, which would consist in becoming, like Daniel Bell, an ideologue of technocracy and an apologist for the system itself. How he does this is to transfer the older ideologies of aesthetic high modernism, the celebration of its revolutionary power, to science and scientific research proper. Now it is the latter's infinite capacity for innovation, change, break, renewal, which will infuse the otherwise repressive system with the disalienating excitement of the new and the "unknown" (the last word of Lyotard's text), as well as of adventure, the refusal of conformity, and the heterogeneities of desire.

Unfortunately, the other conjoined value of the book's conclusion —that of justice—tends, as in all interesting narratives, to return on this one and undermine its seeming certainties. The dynamic of perpetual change is, as Marx showed in the *Manifesto*, not some alien rhythm within capital—a rhythm specific to those noninstrumental activities that are art and science—but rather is the very "permanent revolution" of capitalist production itself: at which point the exhilaration with such revolutionary dynamism is a feature of the bonus of pleasure and the reward of the social reproduction of the system itself. The moment of truth, in this respect, comes when the matter of the ownership and control of the new information banks—the profitability of the new technological and information revolution—returns in these last pages with a vengeance: the dystopian prospect of a global private monopoly of information weighs heavily in the balance against the pleasures of paralogisms and of "anarchist science" (Feyerabend). Yet that monopoly, like the rest of the private property system, cannot be expected to be reformed by however benign a technocratic elite, but can be challenged only by genuinely political (and not symbolic or protopolitical) action.

Notes

1. See for example Lovis Althusser's essays in epistemology or, in another national tradition, Richard Rorty's *Philosophy and the Mirror of Nature* (Princeton: Princeton University Press, 1979) and his *Consequences of Pragmatism* (Minneapolis: University of Minnesota Press, 1982).

2. See his interesting memoir, "Pierre Souyri, Le Marxisme qui n'a pas fini," in *Esprit* 61 (January 1982): 11-31.

3. Jürgen Habermas, *Legitimation Crisis*, trans. Thomas McCarthy (Boston: Beacon Press, 1975), p. 105. And see also his more recent *Zur Rekonstruktion des Historischen*

Materialismus (Frankfurt: Suhrkamp Verlag, 1981), in which the transformation of society is viewed in terms of Piagetian evolutionary stages: paradoxically the problem here is also that of Lyotard when he confronts the monopolization of information by multinational corporations today—namely that there is no reason to believe such a situation can be solved by peaceful evolution or by rational persuasion.

4. Ernest Mandel, *Late Capitalism* (London: New Left Books, 1975), pp. 190-91.

5. See his "Response à la question: qu-est-ce que le postmoderne?" in *Critique,* April 1982, pp. 357-67, which is included in this book as an appendix; as well as his interesting book on Marcel Duchamp, *Les Transformateurs Duchamp* (Paris: Galilee, 1977).

6. See his "Modernity versus Postmodernity," in *New German Critique* 22 (Winter 1981): 3-14.

7. See for a useful discussion of current postmodernist theories of architecture, Paolo Portoghesi, *After Modern Architecture* (New York: Rizzoli, 1982).

8. *Anti-Oedipus: Capitalism and Schizophrenia,* trans. Robert Hurley, Mark Seem, and Helen R. Lane, with preface by Michel Foucault (Minneapolis: University of Minnesota Press, 1983; reprint of 1977 Viking edition), pp. 456-57.

9. See "De la force des faibles," in special Lyotard issue of *L'Arc* 64 (1976): 4-12.

Introduction

The object of this study is the condition of knowledge in the most highly developed societies. I have decided to use the word *postmodern* to describe that condition. The word is in current use on the American continent among sociologists and critics; it designates the state of our culture following the transformations which, since the end of the nineteenth century, have altered the game rules for science, literature, and the arts. The present study will place these transformations in the context of the crisis of narratives.

Science has always been in conflict with narratives. Judged by the yardstick of science, the majority of them prove to be fables. But to the extent that science does not restrict itself to stating useful regularities and seeks the truth, it is obliged to legitimate the rules of its own game. It then produces a discourse of legitimation with respect to its own status, a discourse called philosophy. I will use the term *modern* to designate any science that legitimates itself with reference to a metadiscourse of this kind making an explicit appeal to some grand narrative, such as the dialectics of Spirit, the hermeneutics of meaning, the emancipation of the rational or working subject, or the creation of wealth. For example, the rule of consensus between the sender and addressee of a statement with truth-value is deemed acceptable if it is cast in terms of a possible unanimity between rational minds: this is the Enlightenment narrative, in which the hero of knowledge works toward a good ethico-political end — universal peace. As can be seen from this example, if a metanarrative implying a philosophy of history is used to legitimate knowledge, questions are raised concerning the validity of the institutions governing the social bond: these must be legitimated as well. Thus justice is consigned to the grand narrative in the same way as truth.

Simplifying to the extreme, I define *postmodern* as incredulity toward metanarratives. This incredulity is undoubtedly a product of progress in the sciences: but that progress in turn presupposes it. To the obsolescence of the metanarrative apparatus of legitimation corresponds, most notably, the crisis of metaphysical philosophy and of the university institution which in the past relied on it. The narrative function is losing its functors, its great hero, its great dangers, its great voyages, its great goal. It is being dispersed in clouds of narrative language elements — narrative, but also denotative, prescriptive, descriptive, and so on. Conveyed within each cloud are pragmatic valencies specific to its kind. Each of us lives at the intersection of many of these. However, we do not necessarily establish stable language combinations, and the properties of the ones we do establish are not necessarily communicable.

Thus the society of the future falls less within the province of a Newtonian anthropology (such as stucturalism or systems theory) than a pragmatics of language particles. There are many different language games — a heterogeneity of elements. They only give rise to institutions in patches — local determinism.

The decision makers, however, attempt to manage these clouds of sociality according to input/output matrices, following a logic which implies that their elements are commensurable and that the whole is determinable. They allocate our lives for the growth of power. In matters of social justice and of scientific truth alike, the legitimation of that power is based on its optimizing the system's performance — efficiency. The application of this criterion to all of our games necessarily entails a certain level of terror, whether soft or hard: be operational (that is, commensurable) or disappear.

The logic of maximum performance is no doubt inconsistent in many ways, particularly with respect to contradiction in the socio-economic field: it demands both less work (to lower production costs) and more (to lessen the social burden of the idle population). But our incredulity is now such that we no longer expect salvation to rise from these inconsistencies, as did Marx.

Still, the postmodern condition is as much a stranger to disenchantment as it is to the blind positivity of delegitimation. Where, after the metanarratives, can legitimacy reside? The operativity criterion is technological; it has no relevance for judging what is true or just. Is legitimacy to be found in consensus obtained through discussion, as Jürgen Habermas thinks? Such consensus does violence to the heterogeneity of language games. And invention is always born of dissension. Postmodern knowledge is not simply a tool of the authorities; it refines our sensitivity to differences and reinforces our ability to tolerate the incommensurable. Its principle is not the expert's homology, but the inventor's paralogy.

Here is the question: is a legitimation of the social bond, a just society, feasible in terms of a paradox analogous to that of scientific activity? What would such a paradox be?

The text that follows is an occasional one. It is a report on knowledge in the most highly developed societies and was presented to the Conseil des Universitiés of the government of Quebec at the request of its president. I would like to thank him for his kindness in allowing its publication.

It remains to be said that the author of the report is a philosopher, not an expert. The latter knows what he knows and what he does not know: the former does not. One concludes, the other questions—two very different language games. I combine them here with the result that neither quite succeeds.

The philosopher at least can console himself with the thought that the formal and pragmatic analysis of certain philosophical and ethico-political discourses of legitimation, which underlies the report, will subsequently see the light of day. The report will have served to introduce that analysis from a somewhat sociologizing slant, one that truncates but at the same time situates it.

Such as it is, I dedicate this report to the Institut Polytechnique de Philosophie of the Université de Paris VIII (Vincennes)—at this very postmodern moment that finds the University nearing what may be its end, while the Institute may just be beginning.

The Postmodern Condition

The Postmodern Condition

1. The Field: Knowledge in Computerized Societies

Our working hypothesis is that the status of knowledge is altered as societies enter what is known as the postindustrial age and cultures enter what is known as the postmodern age.[1] This transition has been under way since at least the end of the 1950s, which for Europe marks the completion of reconstruction. The pace is faster or slower depending on the country, and within countries it varies according to the sector of activity: the general situation is one of temporal disjunction which makes sketching an overview difficult.[2] A portion of the description would necessarily be conjectural. At any rate, we know that it is unwise to put too much faith in futurology.[3]

Rather than painting a picture that would inevitably remain incomplete, I will take as my point of departure a single feature, one that immediately defines our object of study. Scientific knowledge is a kind of discourse. And it is fair to say that for the last forty years the "leading" sciences and technologies have had to do with language: phonology and theories of linguistics,[4] problems of communication and cybernetics,[5] modern theories of algebra and informatics,[6] computers and their languages,[7] problems of translation and the search for areas of compatibility among computer languages,[8] problems of information storage and data banks,[9] telematics and the perfection of intelligent terminals,[10] paradoxology.[11] The facts speak for themselves (and this list is not exhaustive).

These technological transformations can be expected to have a considerable impact on knowledge. Its two principal functions—research and the transmission of acquired learning—are already feeling the effect, or will in the future. With respect to the first function, genetics provides an example that is accessible to the layman: it owes its theoretical paradigm to cybernetics. Many other examples could be cited. As for the second function, it is common knowledge that the miniaturization and commercialization of machines is already changing the way in which learning is acquired, classified, made available, and exploited.[12] It is reasonable to suppose that the proliferation of information-processing machines is having, and will continue to have, as much of an effect on the circulation of learning as did advancements in human circulation (transportation systems) and later, in the circulation of sounds and visual images (the media).[13]

The nature of knowledge cannot survive unchanged within this context of general transformation. It can fit into the new channels, and become operational, only if learning is translated into quantities of information.[14] We can predict that anything in the constituted body of knowledge that is not translatable in this way will be abandoned and that the direction of new research will be dictated by the possibility of its eventual results being translatable into computer language. The "producers" and users of knowledge must now, and will have to, possess the means of translating into these languages whatever they want to invent or learn. Research on translating machines is already well advanced.[15] Along with the hegemony of computers comes a certain logic, and therefore a certain set of prescriptions determining which statements are accepted as "knowledge" statements.

We may thus expect a thorough exteriorization of knowledge with respect to the "knower," at whatever point he or she may occupy in the knowledge process. The old principle that the acquisition of knowledge is indissociable from the training (*Bildung*) of minds, or even of individuals, is becoming obsolete and will become ever more so. The relationship of the suppliers and users of knowledge to the knowledge they supply and use is now tending, and will increasingly tend, to assume the form already taken by the relationship of commodity producers and consumers to the commodities they produce and consume—that is, the form of value. Knowledge is and will be produced in order to be sold, it is and will be consumed in order to be valorized in a new production: in both cases, the goal is exchange.

Knowledge ceases to be an end in itself, it loses its "use-value."[16]

It is widely accepted that knowledge has become the principle force of production over the last few decades;[17] this has already had a noticeable effect on the composition of the work force of the most highly developed countries[18] and constitutes the major bottleneck for the developing countries. In the postindustrial and postmodern age, science will maintain and no doubt strengthen its preeminence in the arsenal of productive capacities of the nation-states. Indeed, this situation is one of the reasons leading to the conclusion that the gap between developed and developing countries will grow ever wider in the future.[19]

But this aspect of the problem should not be allowed to overshadow the other, which is complementary to it. Knowledge in the form of an informational commodity indispensable to productive power is already, and will continue to be, a major – perhaps *the* major – stake in the worldwide competition for power. It is conceivable that the nation-states will one day fight for control of information, just as they battled in the past for control over territory, and afterwards for control of access to and exploitation of raw materials and cheap labor. A new field is opened for industrial and commercial strategies on the one hand, and political and military strategies on the other.[20]

However, the perspective I have outlined above is not as simple as I have made it appear. For the mercantilization of knowledge is bound to affect the privilege the nation-states have enjoyed, and still enjoy, with respect to the production and distribution of learning. The notion that learning falls within the purview of the State, as the brain or mind of society, will become more and more outdated with the increasing strength of the opposing principle, according to which society exists and progresses only if the messages circulating within it are rich in information and easy to decode. The ideology of communicational "transparency," which goes hand in hand with the commercialization of knowledge, will begin to perceive the State as a factor of opacity and "noise." It is from this point of view that the problem of the relationship between economic and State powers threatens to arise with a new urgency.

Already in the last few decades, economic powers have reached the point of imperiling the stability of the State through new forms of the circulation of capital that go by the generic name of *multinational corporations*. These new forms of circulation imply that investment decisions have, at least in part, passed beyond the control of the nation-states.[21] The question threatens to become even more thorny with the development of computer technology and telematics. Suppose, for example, that a firm such as IBM is authorized to occupy a belt in the earth's orbital field and launch communications satellites or satellites housing data banks. Who will have access to them? Who will determine which channels or data are forbidden? The State? Or will the State simply be one user among others? New legal issues will be raised, and with them the question: "who will know?"

Transformation in the nature of knowledge, then, could well have repercussions on the existing public powers, forcing them to reconsider their relations (both de jure and de facto) with the large corporations and, more generally, with civil society. The reopening of the world market, a return to vigorous economic competition, the breakdown of the hegemony of American capitalism, the decline of the socialist alternative, a probable opening of the Chinese market— these and many other factors are already, at the end of the 1970s, preparing States for a serious reappraisal of the role they have been accustomed to playing since the 1930s: that of guiding, or even directing investments.[22] In this light, the new technologies can only increase the urgency of such a reexamination, since they make the information used in decision making (and therefore the means of control) even more mobile and subject to piracy.

It is not hard to visualize learning circulating along the same lines as money, instead of for its "educational" value or political (administrative, diplomatic, military) importance; the pertinent distinction would no longer be between knowledge and ignorance, but rather, as is the case with money, between "payment knowledge" and "investment knowledge"—in other words, between units of knowledge exchanged in a daily maintenance framework (the reconstitution of the work force, "survival") versus funds of knowledge dedicated to optimizing the performance of a project.

If this were the case, communicational transparency would be similar to liberalism. Liberalism does not preclude an organization of the flow of money in which some channels are used in decision making while others are only good for the payment of debts. One could similarly imagine flows of knowledge traveling along identical channels of identical nature, some of which would be reserved for the "decision makers," while the others would be used to repay each person's perpetual debt with respect to the social bond.

2. The Problem: Legitimation

That is the working hypothesis defining the field within which I intend to consider the question of the status of knowledge. This

scenario, akin to the one that goes by the name "the computerization of society" (although ours is advanced in an entirely different
spirit), makes no claims of being original, or even true. What is
required of a working hypothesis is a fine capacity for discrimination. The scenario of the computerization of the most highly developed societies allows us to spotlight (though with the risk of excessive
magnification) certain aspects of the transformation of knowledge
and its effects on public power and civil institutions—effects it
would be difficult to perceive from other points of view. Our hypothesis, therefore, should not be accorded predictive value in relation to
reality, but strategic value in relation to the question raised.

Nevertheless, it has strong credibility, and in that sense our choice
of this hypothesis is not arbitrary. It has been described extensively
by the experts[23] and is already guiding certain decisions by the
governmental agencies and private firms most directly concerned,
such as those managing the telecommunications industry. To some
extent, then, it is already a part of observable reality. Finally, barring
economic stagnation or a general recession (resulting, for example,
from a continued failure to solve the world's energy problems),
there is a good chance that this scenario will come to pass: it is hard
to see what other direction contemporary technology could take as
an alternative to the computerization of society.

This is as much as to say that the hypothesis is banal. But only to
the extent that it fails to challenge the general paradigm of progress
in science and technology, to which economic growth and the expansion of sociopolitical power seem to be natural complements. That
scientific and technical knowledge is cumulative is never questioned.
At most, what is debated is the form that accumulation takes—some
picture it as regular, continuous, and unanimous, others as periodic,
discontinuous, and conflictual.[24]

But these truisms are fallacious. In the first place, scientific knowledge does not represent the totality of knowledge; it has always
existed in addition to, and in competition and conflict with, another
kind of knowledge, which I will call narrative in the interests of
simplicity (its characteristics will be described later). I do not mean
to say that narrative knowledge can prevail over science, but its
model is related to ideas of internal equilibrium and conviviality[25]
next to which contemporary scientific knowledge cuts a poor figure,
especially if it is to undergo an exteriorization with respect to the
"knower" and an alienation from its user even greater than has
previously been the case. The resulting demoralization of researchers
and teachers is far from negligible; it is well known that during the
1960s, in all of the most highly developed societies, it reached such

explosive dimensions among those preparing to practice these professions—the students—that there was noticeable decrease in productivity at laboratories and universities unable to protect themselves from
its contamination.[26] Expecting this, with hope or fear, to lead to a
revolution (as was then often the case) is out of the question: it will
not change the order of things in postindustrial society overnight.
But this doubt on the part of scientists must be taken into account as
a major factor in evaluating the present and future status of scientific
knowledge.

It is all the more necessary to take it into consideration since—and
this is the second point—the scientists' demoralization has an impact
on the central problem of legitimation. I use the word in a broader
sense than do contemporary German theorists in their discussions of
the question of authority.[27] Take any civil law as an example: it
states that a given category of citizens must perform a specific kind
of action. Legitimation is the process by which a legislator is authorized to promulgate such a law as a norm. Now take the example of a
scientific statement: it is subject to the rule that a statement must
fulfill a given set of conditions in order to be accepted as scientific.
In this case, legitimation is the process by which a "legislator" dealing with scientific discourse is authorized to prescribe the stated
conditions (in general, conditions of internal consistency and experimental verification) determining whether a statement is to be included
in that discourse for consideration by the scientific community.

The parallel may appear forced. But as we will see, it is not. The
question of the legitimacy of science has been indissociably linked to
that of the legitimation of the legislator since the time of Plato.
From this point of view, the right to decide what is true is not independent of the right to decide what is just, even if the statements
consigned to these two authorities differ in nature. The point is that
there is a strict interlinkage between the kind of language called
science and the kind called ethics and politics: they both stem from
the same perspective, the same "choice" if you will—the choice
called the Occident.

When we examine the current status of scientific knowledge—at a
time when science seems more completely subordinated to the prevailing powers than ever before and, along with the new technologies,
is in danger of becoming a major stake in their conflicts—the question of double legitimation, far from receding into the background,
necessarily comes to the fore. For it appears in its most complete
form, that of reversion, revealing that knowledge and power are

simply two sides of the same question: who decides what knowledge is, and who knows what needs to be decided? In the computer age, the question of knowledge is now more than ever a question of government.

3. The Method: Language Games

The reader will already have noticed that in analyzing this problem within the framework set forth I have favored a certain procedure: emphasizing facts of language and in particular their pragmatic aspect.[28] To help clarify what follows it would be useful to summarize, however briefly, what is meant here by the term *pragmatic*.

A denotative utterance[29] such as "The university is sick," made in the context of a conversation or an interview, positions its sender (the person who utters the statement), its addressee (the person who receives it), and its referent (what the statement deals with) in a specific way: the utterance places (and exposes) the sender in the position of "knower" (he knows what the situation is with the university), the addressee is put in the position of having to give or refuse his assent, and the referent itself is handled in a way unique to denotatives, as something that demands to be correctly identified and expressed by the statement that refers to it.

If we consider a declaration such as "The university is open," pronounced by a dean or rector at convocation, it is clear that the previous specifications no longer apply. Of course, the meaning of the utterance has to be understood, but that is a general condition of communication and does not aid us in distinguishing the different kinds of utterances or their specific effects. The distinctive feature of this second, "performative,"[30] utterance is that its effect upon the referent coincides with its enunciation. The university is open because it has been declared open in the above-mentioned circumstances. That this is so is not subject to discussion or verification on the part of the addressee, who is immediately placed within the new context created by the utterance. As for the sender, he must be invested with the authority to make such a statement. Actually, we could say it the other way around: the sender is dean or rector—that is, he is invested with the authority to make this kind of statement—only insofar as he can directly affect both the referent, (the university) and the addressee (the university staff) in the manner I have indicated.

A different case involves utterances of the type, "Give money to the university"; these are prescriptions. They can be modulated as orders, commands, instructions, recommendations, requests, prayers, pleas, etc. Here, the sender is clearly placed in a position of authority, using the term broadly (including the authority of a sinner over a god who claims to be merciful): that is, he expects the addressee to perform the action referred to. The pragmatics of prescription entail concomitant changes in the posts of addressee and referent.[31]

Of a different order again is the efficiency of a question, a promise, a literary description, a narration, etc. I am summarizing. Wittgenstein, taking up the study of language again from scratch, focuses his attention on the effects of different modes of discourse; he calls the various types of utterances he identifies along the way (a few of which I have listed) *language games*.[32] What he means by this term is that each of the various categories of utterance can be defined in terms of rules specifying their properties and the uses to which they can be put—in exactly the same way as the game of chess is defined by a set of rules determining the properties of each of the pieces, in other words, the proper way to move them.

It is useful to make the following three observations about language games. The first is that their rules do not carry within themselves their own legitimation, but are the object of a contract, explicit or not, between players (which is not to say that the players invent the rules). The second is that if there are no rules, there is no game,[33] that even an infinitesimal modification of one rule alters the nature of the game, that a "move" or utterance that does not satisfy the rules does not belong to the game they define. The third remark is suggested by what has just been said: every utterance should be thought of as a "move" in a game.

This last observation brings us to the first principle underlying our method as a whole: to speak is to fight, in the sense of playing, and speech acts[34] fall within the domain of a general agonistics.[35] This does not necessarily mean that one plays in order to win. A move can be made for the sheer pleasure of its invention: what else is involved in that labor of language harassment undertaken by popular speech and by literature? Great joy is had in the endless invention of turns of phrase, of words and meanings, the process behind the evolution of language on the level of *parole*. But undoubtedly even this pleasure depends on a feeling of success won at the expense of an adversary—at least one adversary, and a formidable one: the accepted language, or connotation.[36]

This idea of an agonistics of language should not make us lose sight of the second principle, which stands as a complement to it

and governs our analysis: that the observable social bond is composed of language "moves." An elucidation of this proposition will
take us to the heart of the matter at hand.

4. The Nature of the Social Bond: The Modern Alternative

If we wish to discuss knowledge in the most highly developed contemporary society, we must answer the preliminary question of what
methodological representation to apply to that society. Simplifying
to the extreme, it is fair to say that in principle there have been, at
least over the last half-century, two basic representational models for
society: either society forms a functional whole, or it is divided in
two. An illustration of the first model is suggested by Talcott Parsons
(at least the postwar Parsons) and his school, and of the second, by
the Marxist current (all of its component schools, whatever differences they may have, accept both the principle of class struggle and
dialectics as a duality operating within society).[37]

This methodological split, which defines two major kinds of discourse on society, has been handed down from the nineteenth
century. The idea that society forms an organic whole, in the absence
of which it ceases to be a society (and sociology ceases to have an
object of study), dominated the minds of the founders of the French
school. Added detail was supplied by functionalism; it took yet
another turn in the 1950s with Parsons's conception of society as a
self-regulating system. The theoretical and even material model is
no longer the living organism; it is provided by cybernetics, which,
during and after the Second World War, expanded the model's
applications.

In Parsons's work, the principle behind the system is still, if I
may say so, optimistic: it corresponds to the stabilization of the
growth economies and societies of abundance under the aegis of a
moderate welfare state.[38] In the work of contemporary German
theorists, *systemtheorie* is technocratic, even cynical, not to mention despairing: the harmony between the needs and hopes of
individuals or groups and the functions guaranteed by the system is
now only a secondary component of its functioning. The true goal
of the system, the reason it programs itself like a computer, is the
optimization of the global relationship between input and output—
in other words, performativity. Even when its rules are in the process
of changing and innovations are occurring, even when its dysfunc-
tions (such as strikes, crises, unemployment, or political revolutions)
inspire hope and lead to belief in an alternative, even then what is

actually taking place is only an internal readjustment, and its result can be no more than an increase in the system's "viability." The only alternative to this kind of performance improvement is entropy, or decline.[39]

Here again, while avoiding the simplifications inherent in a sociology of social theory, it is difficult to deny at least a parallel between this "hard" technocratic version of society and the ascetic effort that was demanded (the fact that it was done in name of "advanced liberalism" is beside the point) of the most highly developed industrial societies in order to make them competitive—and thus optimize their "rationality"—within the framework of the resumption of economic world war in the 1960s.

Even taking into account the massive displacement intervening between the thought of a man like Comte and the thought of Luhmann, we can discern a common conception of the social: society is a unified totality, a "unicity." Parsons formulates this clearly: "The most essential condition of successful dynamic analysis is a continual and systematic reference of every problem to the state of the system as a whole. . . . A process or set of conditions either 'contributes' to the maintenance (or development) of the system or it is 'dysfunctional' in that it detracts from the integration, effectiveness, etc., of the system."[40] The "technocrats"[41] also subscribe to this idea. Whence its credibility: it has the means to become a reality, and that is all the proof it needs. This is what Horkheimer called the "paranoia" of reason.[42]

But this realism of systemic self-regulation, and this perfectly sealed circle of facts and interpretations, can be judged paranoid only if one has, or claims to have, at one's disposal a viewpoint that is in principle immune from their allure. This is the function of the principle of class struggle in theories of society based on the work of Marx.

"Traditional" theory is always in danger of being incorporated into the programming of the social whole as a simple tool for the optimization of its performance; this is because its desire for a unitary and totalizing truth lends itself to the unitary and totalizing practice of the system's managers. "Critical" theory,[43] based on a principle of dualism and wary of syntheses and reconciliations, should be in a position to avoid this fate. What guides Marxism, then, is a different model of society, and a different conception of the function of the knowledge that can be produced by society and acquired from it. This model was born of the struggles accompanying the process of capitalism's encroachment upon traditional civil societies. There is insufficient space here to chart the vicissitudes of these struggles, which fill more than a century of social, political, and ideological history. We will have to content ourselves with a glance at the balance sheet, which is possible for us to tally today now that their fate is known: in countries with liberal or advanced liberal management, the struggles and their instruments have been transformed into regulators of the system; in communist countries, the totalizing model and its totalitarian effect have made a comeback in the name of Marxism itself, and the struggles in question have simply been deprived of the right to exist.[44] Everywhere, the Critique of political economy (the subtitle of Marx's *Capital*) and its correlate, the critique of alienated society, are used in one way or another as aids in programming the system.[45]

Of course, certain minorities, such as the Frankfurt School or the group *Socialisme ou barbarie*,[46] preserved and refined the critical model in opposition to this process. But the social foundation of the principle of division, or class struggle, was blurred to the point of losing all of its radicality; we cannot conceal the fact that the critical model in the end lost its theoretical standing and was reduced to the status of a "utopia" or "hope,"[47] a token protest raised in the name of man or reason or creativity, or again of some social category — such as the Third World or the students[48] — on which is conferred in extremis the henceforth improbable function of critical subject.

The sole purpose of this schematic (or skeletal) reminder has been to specify the problematic in which I intend to frame the question of knowledge in advanced industrial societies. For it is impossible to know what the state of knowledge is — in other words, the problems its development and distribution are facing today — without knowing something of the society within which it is situated. And today more than ever, knowing about that society involves first of all choosing what approach the inquiry will take, and that necessarily means choosing how society can answer. One can decide that the principal role of knowledge is as an indispensable element in the functioning of society, and act in accordance with that decision, only if one has already decided that society is a giant machine.[49]

Conversely, one can count on its critical function, and orient its development and distribution in that direction, only after it has been decided that society does not form an integrated whole, but remains haunted by a principle of opposition.[50] The alternative seems clear: it is a choice between the homogeneity and the intrinsic duality of the social, between functional and critical knowledge. But the decision seems difficult, or arbitrary.

It is tempting to avoid the decision altogether by distinguishing two kinds of knowledge. One, the positivist kind, would be directly applicable to technologies bearing on men and materials, and would lend itself to operating as an indispensable productive force within the system. The other—the critical, reflexive, or hermeneutic kind— by reflecting directly or indirectly on values or aims, would resist any such "recuperation."[51]

5. The Nature of the Social Bond: The Postmodern Perspective

I find this partition solution unacceptable. I suggest that the alternative it attempts to resolve, but only reproduces, is no longer relevant for the societies with which we are concerned and that the solution itself is still caught within a type of oppositional thinking that is out of step with the most vital modes of postmodern knowledge. As I have already said, economic "redeployment" in the current phase of capitalism, aided by a shift in techniques and technology, goes hand in hand with a change in the function of the State: the image of society this syndrome suggests necessitates a serious revision of the alternate approaches considered. For brevity's sake, suffice it to say that functions of regulation, and therefore of reproduction, are being and will be further withdrawn from administrators and entrusted to machines. Increasingly, the central question is becoming who will have access to the information these machines must have in storage to guarantee that the right decisions are made. Access to data is, and will continue to be, the prerogative of experts of all stripes. The ruling class is and will continue to be the class of decision makers. Even now it is no longer composed of the traditional political class, but of a composite layer of corporate leaders, high-level administrators, and the heads of the major professional, labor, political, and religious organizations.[52]

What is new in all of this is that the old poles of attraction represented by nation-states, parties, professions, institutions, and historical traditions are losing their attraction. And it does not look as though they will be replaced, at least not on their former scale. The Trilateral Commission is not a popular pole of attraction. "Identifying" with the great names, the heroes of contemporary history, is becoming more and more difficult.[53] Dedicating oneself to "catching up with Germany," the life goal the French president [Giscard d'Estaing at the time this book was published in France] seems to be offering his countrymen, is not exactly exicting. But then again, it is not exactly a life goal. It depends on each individual's industriousness. Each individual is referred to himself. And each of us knows that our *self* does not amount to much.[54]

This breaking up of the grand Narratives (discussed below, sections 9 and 10) leads to what some authors analyze in terms of the dissolution of the social bond and the disintegration of social aggregates into a mass of individual atoms thrown into the absurdity of Brownian motion.[55] Nothing of the kind is happening: this point of view, it seems to me, is haunted by the paradisaic representation of a lost "organic" society.

A *self* does not amount to much, but no self is an island; each exists in a fabric of relations that is now more complex and mobile than ever before. Young or old, man or woman, rich or poor, a person is always located at "nodal points" of specific communication circuits, however tiny these may be.[56] Or better: one is always located at a post through which various kinds of messages pass. No one, not even the least privileged among us, is ever entirely powerless over the messages that traverse and position him at the post of sender, addressee, or referent. One's mobility in relation to these language game effects (language games, of course, are what this is all about) is tolerable, at least within certain limits (and the limits are vague); it is even solicited by regulatory mechanisms, and in particular by the self-adjustments the system undertakes in order to improve its performance. It may even be said that the system can and must encourage such movement to the extent that it combats its own entropy; the novelty of an unexpected "move," with its correlative displacement of a partner or group of partners, can supply the system with that increased performativity it forever demands and consumes.[57]

It should now be clear from which perspective I chose language games as my general methodological approach. I am not claiming that the *entirety* of social relations is of this nature—that will remain an open question. But there is no need to resort to some fiction of social origins to establish that language games are the minimum relation required for society to exist: even before he is born, if only by virtue of the name he is given, the human child is already positioned as the referent in the story recounted by those around him, in relation to which he will inevitably chart his course.[58] Or more simply still, the question of the social bond, insofar as it is a question, is itself a language game, the game of inquiry. It immediately positions the person who asks, as well as the addressee and the referent asked about: it is already the social bond.

On the other hand, in a society whose communication component is becoming more prominent day by day, both as a reality and as an issue,[59] it is clear that language assumes a new importance. It would be superficial to reduce its significance to the traditional alternative between manipulatory speech and the unilateral transmission of messages on the one hand, and free expression and dialogue on the other.

A word on this last point. If the problem is described simply in terms of communication theory, two things are overlooked: first, messages have quite different forms and effects depending on whether they are, for example, denotatives, prescriptives, evaluatives, performatives, etc. It is clear that what is important is not simply the fact that they communicate information. Reducing them to this function is to adopt an outlook which unduly privileges the system's own interests and point of view. A cybernetic machine does indeed run on information, but the goals programmed into it, for example, originate in prescriptive and evaluative statements it has no way to correct in the course of its functioning—for example, maximizing its own performance. How can one guarantee that performance maximization is the best goal for the social system in every case? In any case the "atoms" forming its matter are competent to handle statements such as these—and this question in particular.

Second, the trivial cybernetic version of information theory misses something of decisive importance, to which I have already called attention: the agonistic aspect of society. The atoms are placed at the crossroads of pragmatic relationships, but they are also displaced by the messages that traverse them, in perpetual motion. Each language partner, when a "move" pertaining to him is made, undergoes a "displacement," an alteration of some kind that not only affects him in his capactiy as addressee and referent, but also as sender. These "moves" necessarily provoke "countermoves"—and everyone knows that a countermove that is merely reactional is not a "good" move. Reactional countermoves are no more than programmed effects in the opponent's strategy; they play into his hands and thus have no effect on the balance of power. That is why it is important to increase displacement in the games, and even to disorient it, in such a way as to make an unexpected "move" (a new statement).

What is needed if we are to understand social relations in this manner, on whatever scale we choose, is not only a theory of communication, but a theory of games which accepts agonistics as a founding principle. In this context, it is easy to see that the essential element of newness is not simply "innovation." Support for this approach can be found in the work of a number of contemporary sociologists,[60] in addition to linguists and philosophers of language.

This "atomization" of the social into flexible networks of language games may seem far removed from the modern reality, which is depicted, on the contrary, as afflicted with bureaucratic paralysis.[61] The objection will be made, at least, that the weight of certain institutions imposes limits on the games, and thus restricts the inventiveness of the players in making their moves. But I think this can be taken into account without causing any particular difficulty.

In the ordinary use of discourse—for example, in a discussion between two friends—the interlocutors use any available ammunition, changing games from one utterance to the next: questions, requests, assertions, and narratives are launched pell-mell into battle. The war is not without rules,[62] but the rules allow and encourage the greatest possible flexibility of utterance.

From this point of view, an institution differs from a conversation in that it always requires supplementary constraints for statements to be declared admissible within its bounds. The constraints function to filter discursive potentials, interrupting possible connections in the communication networks: there are things that should not be said. They also privilege certain classes of statements (sometimes only one) whose predominance characterizes the discourse of the particular institution: there are things that should be said, and there are ways of saying them. Thus: orders in the army, prayer in church, denotation in the schools, narration in families, questions in philosophy, performativity in businesses. Bureaucratization is the outer limit of this tendency.

However, this hypothesis about the institution is still too "unwieldy": its point of departure is an overly "reifying" view of what is institutionalized. We know today that the limits the institution imposes on potential language "moves" are never established once and for all (even if they have been formally defined).[63] Rather, the limits are themselves the stakes and provisional results of language strategies, within the institution and without. Examples: Does the university have a place for language experiments (poetics)? Can you tell stories in a cabinet meeting? Advocate a cause in the barracks? The answers are clear: yes, if the university opens creative workshops; yes, if the cabinet works with prospective scenarios; yes, if the limits of the old institution are displaced.[64] Reciprocally, it can be said that the boundaries only stabilize when they cease to be stakes in the game.

This, I think, is the appropriate approach to contemporary institutions of knowledge.

6. The Pragmatics of Narrative Knowledge

In Section 1, I leveled two objections against the unquestioning acceptance of an instrumental conception of knowledge in the most highly developed societies. Knowledge is not the same as science, especially in its contemporary form; and science, far from successfully obscuring the problem of its legitimacy, cannot avoid raising it with all of its implications, which are no less sociopolitical than epistemological. Let us begin with an analysis of the nature of "narrative" knowledge; by providing a point of comparison, our examination will clarify at least some of the characteristics of the form assumed by scientific knowledge in contemporary society. In addition, it will aid us in understanding how the question of legitimacy is raised or fails to be raised today.

Knowledge, [*savoir*] in general cannot be reduced to science, nor even to learning [*connaissance*]. Learning is the set of statements which, to the exclusion of all other statements, denote or describe objects and may be declared true or false.[65] Science is a subset of learning. It is also composed of denotative statements, but imposes two supplementary conditions on their acceptability: the objects to which they refer must be available for repeated access, in other words, they must be accessible in explicit conditions of observation; and it must be possible to decide whether or not a given statement pertains to the language judged relevant by the experts.[66]

But what is meant by the term *knowledge* is not only a set of denotative statements, far from it. It also includes notions of "know-how," "knowing how to live," "how to listen" [*savoir-faire, savoir-vivre, savoir-écouter*], etc. Knowledge, then, is a question of competence that goes beyond the simple determination and application of the criterion of truth, extending to the determination and application of criteria of efficiency (technical qualification), of justice and/or happiness (ethical wisdom), of the beauty of a sound or color (auditory and visual sensibility), etc. Understood in this way, knowledge is what makes someone capable of forming "good" denotative utterances, but also "good" prescriptive and "good" evaluative utterances. . . . It is not a competence relative to a particular class of statements (for example, cognitive ones) to the exclusion of all others. On the contrary, it makes "good" performances in relation to a variety of objects of discourse possible: objects to be known, decided on, evaluated, transformed. . . . From this derives one of the principal features of knowledge: it coincides with an extensive array of competence-building measures and is the only form embodied in a subject constituted by the various areas of competence composing it.

Another characteristic meriting special attention is the relation between this kind of knowledge and custom. What is a "good" prescriptive or evaluative utterance, a "good" performance in denotative or technical matters? They are all judged to be "good" because they conform to the relevant criteria (of justice, beauty, truth, and efficiency respectively) accepted in the social circle of the "knower's" interlocutors. The early philosophers called this mode of legitimating statements opinion.[67] The consensus that permits such knowledge to be circumscribed and makes it possible to distinguish one who knows from one who doesn't (the foreigner, the child) is what constitutes the culture of a people.[68]

This brief reminder of what knowledge can be in the way of training and culture draws on ethnological description for its justification.[69] But anthropological studies and literature that take rapidly developing societies as their object can attest to the survival of this type of knowledge within them, at least in some of their sectors.[70] The very idea of development presupposes a horizon of nondevelopment where, it is assumed, the various areas of competence remain enveloped in the unity of a tradition and are not differentiated according to separate qualifications subject to specific innovations, debates, and inquiries. This opposition does not necessarily imply a difference in nature between "primitive" and "civilized" man,[71] but is compatible with the premise of a formal identity between "the savage mind" and scientific thought;[72] it is even compatible with the (apparently contrary) premise of the superiority of customary knowledge over the contemporary dispersion of competence.[73]

It is fair to say that there is one point on which all of the investigations agree, regardless of which scenario they propose to dramatize and understand the distance separating the customary state of knowledge from its state in the scientific age: the preeminence of the narrative form in the formulation of traditional knowledge. Some study this form for its own sake;[74] others see it as the diachronic costume of the structural operators that, according to them, properly constitute the knowledge in question;[75] still others bring to it an "economic" interpretation in the Freudian sense of the term.[76] All that is important here is the fact that its form is narrative. Narration is the quintessential form of customary knowledge, in more ways than one.

First, the popular stories themselves recount what could be called positive or negative apprenticeships (*Bildungen*): in other words, the successes or failures greeting the hero's undertakings. These successes or failures either bestow legitimacy upon social institutions (the function of myths), or represent positive or negative models (the successful or unsuccessful hero) of integration into established institutions (legends and tales). Thus the narratives allow the society in which they are told, on the one hand, to define its criteria of competence and, on the other, to evaluate according to those criteria what is performed or can be performed within it.

Second, the narrative form, unlike the developed forms of the discourse of knowledge, lends itself to a great variety of language games. Denotative statements concerning, for example, the state of the sky and the flora and fauna easily slip in; so do deontic statements prescribing what should be done with respect to these same referents, or with respect, to kinship, the difference between the sexes, children, neighbors, foreigners, etc. Interrogative statements are implied, for example, in episodes involving challenges (respond to a question, choose one from a number of things); evaluative statements also enter in, etc. The areas of competence whose criteria the narrative supplies or applies are thus tightly woven together in the web it forms, ordered by the unified viewpoint characteristic of this kind of knowledge.

We shall examine in somewhat more detail a third property, which relates to the transmission of narratives. Their narration usually obeys rules that define the pragmatics of their transmission. I do not mean to say that a given society institutionally assigns the role of narrator to certain categories on the basis of age, sex, or family or professional group. What I am getting at is a pragmatics of popular narratives that is, so to speak, intrinsic to them. For example, a Cashinahua[77] storyteller always begins his narration with a fixed formula: "Here is the story of——, as I've always heard it told. I will tell it to you in my turn. Listen." And he brings it to a close with another, also invariable, formula: "Here ends the story of——. The man who has told it to you is—— (Cashinahua name), or to the Whites—— (Spanish or Portuguese name)."[78]

A quick analysis of this double pragmatic instruction reveals the following: the narrator's only claim to competence for telling the story is the fact that he has heard it himself. The current narratee gains potential access to the same authority simply by listening. It is claimed that the narrative is a faithful transmission (even if the narrative performance is highly inventive) and that it has been told "forever": therefore the hero, a Cashinahuan, was himself once a narratee,

and perhaps a narrator, of the very same story. This similarity of condition allows for the possibility that the current narrator could be
the hero of a narrative, just as the Ancestor was. In fact, he is necessarily
such a hero because he bears a name, declined at the end of his narration,
and that name was given to him in conformity with the canonic narrative
legitimating the assignment of patronyms among the Cashinahua.

The pragmatic rule illustrated by this example cannot, of course,
be universalized.[79] But it gives insight into what is a generally recognized property of traditional knowledge. The narrative "posts"
(sender, addressee, hero) are so organized that the right to occupy
the post of sender receives the following double grounding: it is
based upon the fact of having occupied the post of addressee, and of
having been recounted oneself, by virtue of the name one bears, by a
previous narrative — in other words, having been positioned as the
diegetic reference of other narrative events.[80] The knowledge transmitted by these narrations is in no way limited to the functions of
enunciation; it determines in a single stroke what one must say in
order to be heard, what one must listen to in order to speak, and
what role one must play (on the scene of diegetic reality) to be the
object of a narrative.

Thus the speech acts[81] relevant to this form of knowledge are performed not only by the speaker, but also by the listener, as well as
by the third party referred to. The knowledge arising from such an
apparatus may seem "condensed" in comparison with what I call
"developed" knowledge. Our example clearly illustrates that a narrative tradition is also the tradition of the criteria defining a threefold
competence — "know-how," "knowing how to speak," and "knowing
how to hear" [savoir-faire, savoir-dire, savoir-entendre] — through
which the community's relationship to itself and its environment is
played out. What is transmitted through these narratives is the set of
pragmatic rules that constitutes the social bond.

A fourth aspect of narrative knowledge meriting careful examination is its effect on time. Narrative form follows a rhythm; it is the
synthesis of a meter beating time in regular periods and of accent
modifying the length or amplitude of certain of those periods.[82] This
vibratory, musical property of narrative is clearly revealed in the
ritual performance of certain Cashinahua tales: they are handed
down in initiation ceremonies, in absolutely fixed form, in a language
whose meaning is obscured by lexical and syntactic anomalies, and
they are sung as interminable, monotonous chants.[83] It is a strange
brand of knowledge, you may say, that does not even make itself
understood to the young men to whom it is addressed!

And yet this kind of knowledge is quite common; nursery rhymes are of this type, and repetitive forms of contemporary music have tried to recapture or at least approximate it. It exhibits a surprising feature: as meter takes precedence over accent in the production of sound (spoken or not), time ceases to be a support for memory to become an immemorial beating that, in the absence of a noticeable separation between periods, prevents their being numbered and consigns them to oblivion.[84] Consider the form of popular sayings, proverbs, and maxims: they are like little splinters of potential narratives, or molds of old ones, which have continued to circulate on certain levels of the contemporary social edifice. In their prosody can be recognized the mark of that strange temporalization that jars the golden rule of our knowledge: "never forget."

Now there must be a congruence between this lethal function of narrative knowledge and the functions, cited earlier, of criteria formation, the unification of areas of competence, and social regulation. By way of a simplifying fiction, we can hypothesize that, against all expectations, a collectivity that takes narrative as its key form of competence has no need to remember its past. It finds the raw material for its social bond not only in the meaning of the narratives it recounts, but also in the act of reciting them. The narratives' reference may seem to belong to the past, but in reality it is always contemporaneous with the act of recitation. It is the present act that on each of its occurrences marshals in the ephemeral temporality inhabiting the space between the "I have heard" and the "you will hear."

The important thing about the pragmatic protocol of this kind of narration is that it betokens a theoretical identity between each of the narrative's occurrences. This may not in fact be the case, and often is not, and we should not blind ourselves to the element of humor or anxiety noticeable in the respect this etiquette inspires. The fact remains that what is emphasized is the metrical beat of the narrative occurrences, not each performance's differences in accent. It is in this sense that this mode of temporality can be said to be simultaneously evanescent and immemorial.[85]

Finally, a culture that gives precedence to the narrative form doubtless has no more of a need for special procedures to authorize its narratives than it has to remember its past. It is hard to imagine such a culture first isolating the post of narrator from the others in order to give it a privileged status in narrative pragmatics, then inquiring into what right the narrator (who is thus disconnected from the narratee and diegesis) might have to recount what he recounts, and finally undertaking the analysis or anamnesis of its own legitimacy. It is even harder to imagine it handing over the authority for its narratives to some incomprehensible subject of narration. The narratives themselves have this authority. In a sense, the people are only that which actualizes the narratives: once again, they do this not only by recounting them, but also by listening to them and recounting themselves through them; in other words, by putting them into "play" in their institutions—thus by assigning themselves the posts of narratee and diegesis as well as the post of narrator.

There is, then, an incommensurability between popular narrative pragmatics, which provides immediate legitimation, and the language game known to the West as the question of legitimacy—or rather, legitimacy as a referent in the game of inquiry. Narratives, as we have seen, determine criteria of competence and/or illustrate how they are to be applied. They thus define what has the right to be said and done in the culture in question, and since they are themselves a part of that culture, they are legitimated by the simple fact that they do what they do.

7. The Pragmatics of Scientific Knowledge

Let us attempt to characterize, if only in summary fashion, the classical conception of the pragmatics of scientific knowledge. In the process, we will distinguish between the research game and the teaching game.

Copernicus states that the path of the planets is circular.[86] Whether this proposition is true or false, it carries within it a set of tensions, all of which affect each of the pragmatic posts it brings into play: sender, addressee, and referent. These "tensions" are classes of prescriptions which regulate the admissibility of the statement as "scientific."

First, the sender should speak the truth about the referent, the path of the planets. What does this mean? That on the one hand he is supposed to be able to provide proof of what he says, and on the other hand he is supposed to be able to refute any opposing or contradictory statements concerning the same referent.

Second, it should be possible for the addressee validly to give (or refuse) his assent to the statement he hears. This implies that he is himself a potential sender, since when he formulates his agreement or disagreement he will be subject to the same double requirement (or proof or refutation) that Copernicus was. He is therefore supposed to have, potentially, the same qualities as Copernicus: he is his equal.

But this will only become known when he speaks and under the above conditions. Before that, it will be impossible to say whether or not he is a scientific scholar.

Third, the referent (the path of the planets) of which Copernicus speaks is supposed to be "expressed" by his statement in conformity with what it actually is. But since what it is can only be known through statements of the same order as that of Copernicus, the rule of adequation becomes problematical. What I say is true because I prove that it is—but what proof is there that my proof is true?

The scientific solution of this difficulty consists in the observance of two rules. The first of these is dialectical or even rhetorical in the forensic sense:[87] a referent is that which is susceptible to proof and can be used as evidence in a debate. Not: I can prove something because reality is the way I say it is. But: as long as I can produce proof, it is permissible to think that reality is the way I say it is.[88] The second rule is metaphysical; the same referent cannot supply a plurality of contradictory or inconsistent proofs. Or stated differently: "God" is not deceptive.[89]

These two rules underlie what nineteenth-century science calls verification and twentieth-century science, falsification.[90] They allow a horizon of consensus to be brought to the debate between partners (the sender and the addressee). Not every consensus is a sign of truth; but it is presumed that the truth of a statement necessarily draws a consensus.

That covers research. It should be evident that research appeals to teaching as its necessary complement: the scientists needs an addressee who can in turn become the sender; he needs a partner. Otherwise, the verification of his statements would be impossible, since the nonrenewal of the requisite skills would eventually bring an end to the necessary, contradictory debate. Not only the truth of a scientist's statement, but also his competence, is at stake in that debate. One's competence is never an accomplished fact. It depends on whether or not the statement proposed is considered by one's peers to be worth discussion in a sequence of argumentation and refutation. The truth of the statement and the competence of its sender are thus subject to the collective approval of a group of persons who are competent on an equal basis. Equals are needed and must be created.

Didactics is what ensures that this reproduction takes place. It is different from the dialectical game of research. Briefly, its first presupposition is that the addressee, the student, does not know what the sender knows: obviously, that is why he has something to learn. Its second presupposition is that the student can learn what the sender knows and become an expert whose competence is equal to that of his master.[91] This double requirement supposes a third: that there are statements for which the exchange of arguments and the production of proof constituting the pragmatics of research are considered to have been sufficient, and which can therefore be transmitted through teaching as they stand, in the guise of indisputable truths.

In other words, you teach what you know: such is the expert. But as the student (the addressee of the didactic process) improves his skills, the expert can confide to him what he does not know but is trying to learn (at least if the expert is also involved in research). In this way, the student is introduced to the dialectics of research, or the game of producing scientific knowledge.

If we compare the pragmatics of science to that of narrative knowledge, we note the following properties:

1. Scientific knowledge requires that one language game, denotation, be retained and all others excluded. A statement's truth-value is the criterion determining its acceptability. Of course, we find other classes of statements, such as interrogatives ("How can we explain that . . . ?") and prescriptives ("Take a finite series of elements . . . "). But they are only present as turning points in the dialectical argumentation, which must end in a denotative statement.[92] In this context, then, one is "learned" if one can produce a true statement about a referent, and one is a scientist if one can produce verifiable or falsifiable statements about referents accessible to the experts.

2. Scientific knowledge is in this way set apart from the language games that combine to form the social bond. Unlike narrative knowledge, it is no longer a direct and shared component of the bond. But it is indirectly a component of it, because it develops into a profession and gives rise to institutions, and in modern societies language games consolidate themselves in the form of institutions run by qualified partners (the professional class). The relation between knowledge and society (that is, the sum total of partners in the general agonistics, excluding scientists in their professional capacity) becomes one of mutual exteriority. A new problem appears—that of the relationship between the scientific institution and society. Can this problem be solved by didactics, for example, by the premise that any social atom can acquire scientific competence?

3. Within the bounds of the game of research, the competence required concerns the post of sender alone. There is no particular competence required of the addressee (it is required only in didactics—the student must be intelligent). And there is no competence required

of the referent. Even in the case of the human sciences, where it is an aspect of human conduct, the referent is in principle external to the partners engaged in scientific dialectics. Here, in contrast to the narrative game, a person does not have to know how to be what knowledge says he is.

4. A statement of science gains no validity from the fact of being reported. Even in the case of pedagogy, it is taught only if it is still verifiable in the present through argumentation and proof. In itself, it is never secure from "falsification."[93] The knowledge that has accumulated in the form of already accepted statements can always be challenged. But conversely, any new statement that contradicts a previously approved statement regarding the same referent can be accepted as valid only if it refutes the previous statement by producing arguments and proofs.

5. The game of science thus implies a diachronic temporality, that is, a memory and a project. The current sender of a scientific statement is supposed to be acquainted with previous statements concerning its referent (bibliography) and only proposes a new statement on the subject if it differs from the previous ones. Here, what I have called the "accent" of each performance, and by that token the polemical function of the game, takes precedence over the "meter." This diachrony, which assumes memory and a search for the new, represents in principle a cumulative process. Its "rhythm," or the relationship between accent and meter, is variable.[94]

These properties are well known. But they are worth recalling for two reasons. First, drawing a parallel between science and nonscientific (narrative) knowledge helps us understand, or at least sense, that the former's existence is no more—and no less—necessary than the latter's. Both are composed of sets of statements; the statements are "moves" made by the players within the framework of generally applicable rules; these rules are specific to each particular kind of knowledge, and the "moves" judged to be "good" in one cannot be of the same type as those judged "good" in another, unless it happens that way by chance.

It is therefore impossible to judge the existence or validity of narrative knowledge on the basis of scientific knowledge and vice versa: the relevant criteria are different. All we can do is gaze in wonderment at the diversity of discursive species, just as we do at the diversity of plant or animal species. Lamenting the "loss of meaning" in postmodernity boils down to mourning the fact that knowledge is no longer principally narrative. Such a reaction does not necessarily follow. Neither does an attempt to derive or engender (using operators like development) scientific knowledge from narrative knowledge, as if the former contained the latter in an embryonic state.

Nevertheless, language species, like living species, are interrelated, and their relations are far from harmonious. The second point justifying this quick reminder on the properties of the language game of science concerns, precisely, its relation to narrative knowledge. I have said that narrative knowledge does not give priority to the question of its own legitimation and that it certifies itself in the pragmatics of its own transmission without having recourse to argumentation and proof. This is why its incomprehension of the problems of scientific discourse is accompanied by a certain tolerance: it approaches such discourse primarily as a variant in the family of narrative cultures.[95] The opposite is not true. The scientist questions the validity of narrative statements and concludes that they are never subject to argumentation or proof.[96] He classifies them as belonging to a different mentality: savage, primitive, underdeveloped, backward, alienated, composed of opinions, customs, authority, prejudice, ignorance, ideology. Narratives are fables, myths, legends, fit only for women and children. At best, attempts are made to throw some rays of light into this obscurantism, to civilize, educate, develop.

This unequal relationship is an intrinsic effect of the rules specific to each game. We all know its symptoms. It is the entire history of cultural imperialism from the dawn of Western civilization. It is important to recognize its special tenor, which sets it apart from all other forms of imperialism: it is governed by the demand for legitimation.

8. The Narrative Function and the Legitimation of Knowledge

Today the problem of legitimation is no longer considered a failing of the language game of science. It would be more accurate to say that it has itself been legitimated as a problem, that is, as a heuristic driving force. But this way of dealing with it by reversing the situation is of recent date. Before it came to this point (what some call positivism), scientific knowledge sought other solutions. It is remarkable that for a long time it could not help resorting for its solutions to procedures that, overtly or not, belong to narrative knowledge.

This return of the narrative in the non-narrative, in one form or another, should not be thought of as having been superseded once and for all. A crude proof of this: what do scientists do when they appear on television or are interviewed in the newspapers after making a "discovery"? They recount an epic of knowledge that is in fact wholly unepic. They play by the rules of the narrative game; its influence remains considerable not only on the users of the media, but also on the scientist's sentiments. This fact is neither trivial nor accessory: it concerns the relationship of scientific knowledge to "popular" knowledge, or what is left of it. The state spends large amounts of money to enable science to pass itself off as an epic: the State's own credibility is based on that epic, which it uses to obtain the public consent its decision makers need.[97]

It is not inconceivable that the recourse to narrative is inevitable, at least to the extent that the language game of science desires its statements to be true but does not have the resources to legitimate their truth on its own. If this is the case, it is necessary to admit an irreducible need for history understood, as outlined above—not as a need to remember or to project (a need for historicity, for accent), but on the contrary as a need to forget (a need for *metrum*) (see section 6).

We are anticipating ourselves. But as we proceed we should keep in mind that the apparently obsolete solutions that have been found for the problem of legitimation are not obsolete in principle, but only in their expression; we should not be surprised if we find that they have persisted to this day in other forms. Do not we ourselves, at this moment, feel obliged to mount a narrative of scientific knowledge in the West in order to clarify its status?

The new language game of science posed the problem of its own legitimation at the very beginning—in Plato. This is not the proper place for an exegesis of the passages in the *Dialogues* in which the pragmatics of science is set in motion, either explicitly as a theme or implicitly as a presupposition. The game of dialogue, with its specific requirements, encapsulates that pragmatics, enveloping within itself its two functions of research and teaching. We encounter some of the same rules previously enumerated: argumentation with a view only to consensus (*homologia*); the unicity of the referent as a guarantee for the possibility of agreement; parity between partners; and even an indirect recognition that it is a question of a game and not a destiny, since those who refuse to accept the rules, out of weakness or crudeness, are excluded.[98]

There remains the fact that, given the scientific nature of the game, the question of its own legitimacy must be among those raised in the dialogues. A well-known example of this, which is all the more important since it links this question to that of sociopolitical authority from the start, is to be found in books 6 and 7 of *The Republic*. As we know, the answer, at least part of it, comes in the form of a narrative—the allegory of the cave, which recounts how and why men yearn for narratives and fail to recognize knowledge. Knowledge is thus founded on the narrative of its own martyrdom.

There is more. The legitimation effort, the *Dialogues* of Plato, gives ammunition to narrative by virtue of its own form: each of the dialogues takes the form of a narrative of a scientific discussion. It is of little consequence here that the story of the debate is shown rather than reported, staged rather than narrated,[99] and is therefore more closely related to tragedy than epic. The fact is that the Platonic discourse that inaugurates science is not scientific, precisely to the extent that it attempts to legitimate science. Scientific knowledge cannot know and make known that it is the true knowledge without resorting to the other, narrative, kind of knowledge, which from its point of view is no knowledge at all. Without such recourse it would be in the position of presupposing its own validity and would be stooping to what it condemns: begging the question, proceeding on prejudice. But does it not fall into the same trap by using narrative as its authority?

This is not the place to chart the recurrence of the narrative in the scientific by way of the latter's discourses of legitimation, which include but are not limited to the great ancient, medieval, and classical philosophies. Endless torment. As resolute a philosophy as that of Descartes can only demonstrate the legitimacy of science through what Valéry called the story of a mind,[100] or else in a *Bildungsroman*, which is what the *Discourse on Method* amounts to. Aristotle was doubtless one of the most modern of all in separating the rules to which statements declared scientific must conform (the *Organon*) from the search for their legitimacy in a discourse on Being (the *Metaphysics*). Even more modern was his suggestion that scientific knowledge, including its pretension to express the being of the referent, is composed only of arguments and proofs—in other words, of dialectics.[101]

With modern science, two new features appear in the problematic of legitimation. To begin with, it leaves behind the metaphysical search for a first proof or transcendental authority as a response to the question: "How do you prove the proof?" or, more generally, "Who decides the conditions of truth?" It is recognized that the conditions of truth, in other words, the rules of the game of science, are immanent in that game, that they can only be established within the bonds of a debate that is already scientific in nature, and that there is no other proof that the rules are good than the consensus extended to them by the experts.

Accompanying the modern proclivity to define the conditions of a discourse in a discourse on those conditions is a renewed dignity for narrative (popular) cultures, already noticeable in Renaissance Humanism and variously present in the Enlightenment, the *Sturm und Drang*, German idealist philosophy, and the historical school in France. Narration is no longer an involuntary lapse in the legitimation process. The explicit appeal to narrative in the problematic of knowledge is concomitant with the liberation of the bourgeois classes from the traditional authorities. Narrative knowledge makes a resurgence in the West as a way of solving the problem of legitimating the new authorities. It is natural in a narrative problematic for such a question to solicit the name of a hero as its response: *Who* has the right to decide for society? Who is the subject whose prescriptions are norms for those they obligate?

This way of inquiring into sociopolitical legitimacy combines with the new scientific attitude: the name of the hero is the people, the sign of legitimacy is the people's consensus, and their mode of creating norms is deliberation. The notion of progress is a necessary outgrowth of this. It represents nothing other than the movement by which knowledge is presumed to accumulate—but this movement is extended to the new sociopolitical subject. The people debate among themselves about what is just or unjust in the same way that the scientific community debates about what is true or false; they accumulate civil laws just as scientists accumulate scientific laws; they perfect their rules of consensus just as the scientists produce new "paradigms" to revise their rules in light of what they have learned.[102]

It is clear that what is meant here by "the people" is entirely different from what is implied by traditional narrative knowledge, which, as we have seen, requires to instituting deliberation, no cumulative progression, no pretension to universality; these are the operators of scientific knowledge. It is therefore not at all surprising that the representatives of the new process of legitimation by "the people" should be at the same time actively involved in destroying the traditional knowledge of peoples, perceived from that point forward as minorities or potential separatist movements destined only to spread obscurantism.[103]

We can see too that the real existence of this necessarily abstract subject (it is abstract because it is uniquely modeled on the paradigm of the subject of knowledge—that is, one who sends-receives denotative statements with truth-value to the exclusion of other language games) depends on the institutions within which that subject is supposed to deliberate and decide, and which comprise all or part of the State. The question of the State becomes intimately entwined with that of scientific knowledge.

But it is also clear that this interlocking is many sided. The "people" (the nation, or even humanity), and especially their political institutions, are not content to know — they legislate. That is, they formulate prescriptions that have the status of norms.[104] They therefore exercise their competence not only with respect to denotative utterances concerning what is true, but also prescriptive utterances with pretentions to justice. As already said, what characterizes narrative knowledge, what forms the basis of our conception of it, precisely that it combines both of these kinds of competence, not to mention all the others.

The mode of legitimation we are discussing, which reintroduces narrative as the validity of knowledge, can thus take two routes, depending on whether it represents the subject of the narrative as cognitive or practical, as a hero of knowledge or a hero of liberty. Because of this alternative, not only does the meaning of legitimation vary, but it is already apparent that narrative itself is incapable of describing that meaning adequately.

9. Narratives of the Legitimation of Knowledge

We shall examine two major versions of the narrative of legitimation. One is more political, the other more philosophical; both are of great importance in modern history, in particular in the history of knowledge and its institutions.

The subject of the first of these versions is humanity as the hero of liberty. All peoples have a right to science. If the social subject is not already the subject of scientific knowledge, it is because that has been forbidden by priests and tyrants. The right to science must be reconquered. It is understandable that this narrative would be directed more toward a politics of primary education, rather than of universities and high schools.[105] The educational policy of the French Third Republic powerfully illustrates these presuppositions.

It seems that this narrative finds it necessary to de-emphasize higher education. Accordingly, the measures adopted by Napoleon regarding higher education are generally considered to have been motivated by the desire to produce the administrative and professional skills necessary for the stability of the State.[106] This overlooks the fact that in the context of the narrative of freedom, the State receives its legitimacy not from itself but from the people. So even if imperial politics designated the institutions of higher education as a breeding ground for the officers of the State and secondarily, for the managers of civil society, it did so because the nation as a whole was supposed to win its freedom through the spread of new domains of knowledge to the population, a process to be effected through agencies and professions within which those cadres would fulfill their functions. The same reasoning is a fortiori valid for the foundation of properly scientific institutions. The State resorts to the narrative of freedom every time it assumes direct control over the training of the "people," under the name of the "nation," in order to point them down the path of progress.[107]

With the second narrative of legitimation, the relation between science, the nation, and the State develops quite differently. It first appears with the founding, between 1807 and 1810, of the University of Berlin,[108] whose influence on the organization of higher education in the young countries of the world was to be considerable in the nineteenth and twentieth centuries.

At the time of the University's creation, the Prussian ministry had before it a project conceived by Fichte and counterproposals by Schleiermacher. Wilhelm von Humboldt had to decide the matter and came down on the side of Schleiermacher's more "liberal" option.

Reading Humboldt's report, one may be tempted to reduce his entire approach to the politics of the scientific institution to the famous dictum: "Science for its own sake." But this would be to misunderstood the ultimate aim of his policies, which is guided by the principle of legitimation we are discussing and is very close to the one Schleiermacher elucidates in a more thorough fashion.

Humboldt does indeed declare that science obeys its own rules, that the scientific institution "lives and continually renews itself on its own, with no constraint or determined goal whatsoever." But he adds that the University should orient its constituent element, science, to "the spiritual and moral training of the nation."[109] How can this *Bildung*-effect result from the disinterested pursuit of learning? Are not the State, the nation, the whole of humanity indifferent to knowledge for its own sake? What interests them, as Humboldt admits, is not learning, but "character and action."

The minister's adviser thus faces a major conflict, in some ways reminiscent of the split introduced by the Kantian critique between knowing and willing: it is a conflict between a language game made of denotations answerable only to the criterion of truth, and a language game governing ethical, social, and political practice that necessarily involves decisions and obligations, in other words, utterances expected to be just rather than true and which in the final analysis lie outside the realm of scientific knowledge.

However, the unification of these two sets of discourse is indispensable to the *Bildung* aimed for by Humboldt's project, which consists not only in the acquisition of learning by individuals, but also in the training of a fully legitimated subject of knowledge and society. Humboldt therefore invokes a Spirit (what Fichte calls Life), animated by three ambitions, or better, by a single, threefold aspiration: "that of deriving everything from an original principle" (corresponding to scientific activity), "that of relating everything to an ideal" (governing ethical and social practice), and "that of unifying this principle and this ideal in a single Idea" (ensuring that the scientific search for true causes always coincides with the pursuit of just ends in moral and political life). This ultimate synthesis constitutes the legitimate subject.

Humboldt adds in passing that this triple aspiration naturally inheres in the "intellectual character of the German nation."[110] This is a concession, but a discreet one, to the other narrative, to the idea that the subject of knowledge is the people. But in truth this idea is quite distant from the narrative of the legitimation of knowledge advanced by German idealism. The suspicion that men like Schleiermacher, Humboldt, and even Hegel harbor towards the State is an indication of this. If Schleiermacher fears the narrow nationalism, protectionism, utilitarianism, and positivism that guide the public authorities in matters of science, it is because the principle of science does not reside in those authorities, even indirectly. The subject of knowledge is not the people, but the speculative spirit. It is not embodied, as in France after the Revolution, in a State, but in a System. The language game of legitimation is not state-political, but philosophical.

The great function to be fulfilled by the universities is to "lay open the whole body of learning and expound both the principles and the foundations of all knowledge." For "there is no creative scientific capacity without the speculative spirit."[111] "Speculation" is here the name given the discourse on the legitimation of scientific discourse. Schools are functional; the University is speculative, that is to say, philosophical.[112] Philosophy must restore unity to learning, which has been scattered into separate sciences in laboratories and in preuniversity education; it can only achieve this in a language game that links the sciences together as moments in the becoming of spirit, in other words, which links them in a rational narration, or rather metanarration. Hegel's *Encyclopedia* (1817-27) attempts to realize this project of totalization, which was already present in Fichte and Schelling in the form of the idea of the System.

It is here, in the mechanism of developing a Life that is simultaneously Subject, that we see a return of narrative knowledge. There is a universal "history" of spirit, spirit is "life," and "life" is its own self-presentation and formulation in the ordered knowledge of all of its forms contained in the empirical sciences. The encyclopedia of German idealism is the narration of the "(hi)story" of this life-subject. But what it produces is a metanarrative, for the story's narrator must not be a people mired in the particular positivity of its traditional knowledge, nor even scientists taken as a whole, since they are sequestered in professional frameworks corresponding to their respective specialities.

The narrator must be a metasubject in the process of formulating both the legitimacy of the discourses of the empirical sciences and that of the direct institutions of popular cultures. This metasubject, in giving voice to their common grounding, realizes their implicit goal. It inhabits the speculative University. Positive science and the people are only crude versions of it. The only valid way for the nation-state itself to bring the people to expression is through the mediation of speculative knowledge.

It has been necessary to elucidate the philosophy that legitimated the foundation of the University of Berlin and was meant to be the motor both of its development and the development of contemporary knowledge. As I have said, many countries in the nineteenth and twentieth centuries adopted this university organization as a model for the foundation or reform of their own system of higher education, beginning with the United States.[113] But above all, this philosophy—which is far from dead, especially in university circles[114] —offers a particularly vivid representation of one solution to the problem of the legitimacy of knowledge.

Research and the spread of learning are not justified by invoking a principle of usefulness. The idea is not at all that science should serve the interests of the State and/or civil society. The humanist principle that humanity rises up in dignity and freedom through knowledge is left by the wayside. German idealism has recourse to a metaprinciple that simultaneously grounds the development of learning, of society, and of the State in the realization of the "life" of a Subject, called "divine Life" by Fichte and "Life of the spirit" by Hegel. In this perspective, knowledge first finds legitimacy within itself, and it is knowledge that is entitled to say what the State and what Society are.[115] But it can only play this role by changing levels, by ceasing to be simply the positive knowledge of its referent (nature, society, the State, etc.), becoming in addition to that the knowledge of the knowledge of the referent—that is, by becoming speculative. In the names "Life" and "Spirit," knowledge names itself.

A noteworthy result of the speculative apparatus is that all of the discourses of learning about every possible referent are taken up not from the point of view of their immediate truth-value, but in terms of the value they acquire by virtue of occupying a certain place in the itinerary of Spirit or Life—or, if preferred, a certain position in the Encyclopedia recounted by speculative discourse. That discourse cites them in the process of expounding for itself what it knows, that is, in the process of self-exposition. True knowledge, in this perspective, is always indirect knowledge; it is composed of reported statements that are incorporated into the metanarrative of a subject that guarantees their legitimacy.

The same thing applies for every variety of discourse, even if it is not a discourse of learning; examples are the discourse of law and that of the State. Contemporary hermeneutic discourse[116] is born of this presupposition, which guarantees that there is meaning to know and thus confers legitimacy upon history (and especially the history of learning). Statements are treated as their own autonyms[117] and set in motion in a way that is supposed to render them mutually engendering: these are the rules of speculative language. The University, as its name indicates, is its exclusive institution.

But, as I have said, the problem of legitimacy can be solved using the other procedures as well. The difference between them should be kept in mind: today, with the status of knowledge unbalanced and its speculative unity broken, the first version of legitimacy is gaining new vigor.

According to this version, knowledge finds its validity not within itself, not in a subject that develops by actualizing its learning possibilities, but in a practical subject—humanity. The principle of the movement animating the people is not the self-legitimation of knowledge, but the self-grounding of freedom or, if preferred, its self-management. The subject is concrete, or supposedly so, and its epic is the story of its emancipation from everything that prevents it from governing itself. It is assumed that the laws it makes for itself are just, not because they conform to some outside nature, but because the legislators are, constitutionally, the very citizens who are subject to the laws. As a result, the legislator's will—the desire that the laws be just—will always coincide with the will of the citizen, who desires the law and will therefore obey it.

Clearly, this mode of legitimation through the autonomy of the will[118] gives priority to a totally different language game, which Kant called imperative and is known today as prescriptive. The important thing is not, or not only, to legitimate denotative utterances pertaining to the truth, such as "The earth revolves around the sun," but rather to legitimate prescriptive utterances pertaining to justice, such as "Carthage must be destroyed" or "The minimum wage must be set at x dollars." In this context, the only role positive knowledge can play is to inform the practical subject about the reality within which the execution of the prescription is to be inscribed. It allows the subject to circumscribe the executable, or what it is possible to do. But the executory, what should be done, is not within the purview of positive knowledge. It is one thing for an undertaking to be possible and another for it to be just. Knowledge is no longer the subject, but in the service of the subject: its only legitimacy (though it is formidable) is the fact that it allows morality to become reality.

This introduces a relation of knowledge to society and the State which is in principle a relation of the means to the end. But scientists must cooperate only if they judge that the politics of the State, in other words the sum of its prescriptions, is just. If they feel that the civil society of which they are members is badly represented by the State, they may reject its prescriptions. This type of legitimation grants them the authority, as practical human beings, to refuse their scholarly support to a political power they judge to be unjust, in other words, not grounded in a real autonomy. They can even go so far as to use their expertise to demonstrate that such autonomy is not in fact realized in society and the State. This reintroduces the critical function of knowledge. But the fact remains that knowledge has no final legitimacy outside of serving the goals envisioned by the practical subject, the autonomous collectivity.[119]

This distribution of roles in the enterprise of legitimation is interesting from our point of view because it assumes, as against the system-subject theory, that there is no possibility that language games can be unified or totalized in any metadiscourse. Quite to the contrary, here the priority accorded prescriptive statements—uttered by the practical subject—renders them independent in principle from the statements of science, whose only remaining function is to supply this subject with information.

Two remarks:

1. It would be easy to show that Marxism has wavered between the two models of narrative legitimation I have just described. The Party takes the place of the University, the proletariat that of the

people or of humanity, dialectical materialism that of speculative idealism, etc. Stalinism may be the result, with its specific relationship with the sciences: in Stalinism, the sciences only figure as citations from the metanarrative of the march towards socialism, which is the equivalent of the life of the spirit. But on the other hand Marxism can, in conformity to the second version, develop into a form of critical knowledge by declaring that socialism is nothing other than the constitution of the autonomous subject and that the only justification for the sciences is if they give the empirical subject (the proletariat) the means to emancipate itself from alienation and repression: this was, briefly, the position of the Frankfurt School.

2. The speech Heidegger gave on May 27, 1933, on becoming rector of the university of Freiburg-in-Breisgau,[120] can be read as an unfortunate episode in the history of legitimation. Here, speculative science has become the questioning of being. This questioning is the "destiny" of the German people, dubbed an "historico-spiritual people." To this subject are owed the three services of labor, defense, and knowledge. The University guarantees a metaknowledge of the three services, that is to say, science. Here, as in idealism, legitimation is achieved through a metadiscourse called science, with ontological pretensions. But here the metadiscourse is questioning, not totalizing. And the University, the home of this metadiscourse, owes its knowledge to a people whose "historic mission" is to bring that metadiscourse to fruition by working, fighting, and knowing. The calling of this people-subject is not to emancipate humanity, but to realize its "true world of the spirit," which is "the most profound power of conservation to be found within its forces of earth and blood." This insertion of the narrative of race and work into that of the spirit as a way of legitimating knowledge and its institutions is doubly unfortunate: theoretically inconsistent, it was compelling enough to find disastrous echoes in the realm of politics.

10. Delegitimation

In contemporary society and culture—postindustrial society, postmodern culture[121]—the question of the legitimation of knowledge is formulated in different terms. The grand narrative has lost its credibility, regardless of what mode of unification it uses, regardless of whether it is a speculative narrative or a narrative of emancipation.

The decline of narrative can be seen as an effect of the blossoming of techniques and technologies since the Second World War, which has shifted emphasis from the ends of action to its means; it can also

be seen as an effect of the redeployment of advanced liberal capitalism after its retreat under the protection of Keynesianism during the
period 1930-60, a renewal that has eliminated the communist alternative and valorized the individual enjoyment of goods and services.

Anytime we go searching for causes in this way we are bound to
be disappointed. Even if we adopted one or the other of these
hypotheses, we would still have to detail the correlation between the
tendencies mentioned and the decline of the unifying and legitimating power of the grand narratives of speculation and emancipation.

It is, of course, understandable that both capitalist renewal and
prosperity and the disorienting upsurge of technology would have an
impact on the status of knowledge. But in order to understand how
contemporary science could have been susceptible to those effects
long before they took place, we must first locate the seeds of "delegitimation"[122] and nihilism that were inherent in the grand narratives
of the nineteenth century.

First of all, the speculative apparatus maintains an ambigious relation to knowledge. It shows that knowledge is only worthy of that
name to the extent that it reduplicates itself ("lifts itself up," *hebt
sich auf;* is sublated) by citing its own statements in a second-level
discourse (autonymy) that functions to legitimate them. This is as
much as to say that, in its immediacy, denotative discourse bearing
on a certain referent (a living organism, a chemical property, a physical phenomenon, etc.) does not really know what it thinks it knows.
Positive science is not a form of knowledge. And speculation feeds
on its suppression. The Hegelian speculative narrative thus harbors a
certain skepticism toward positive learning, as Hegel himself admits.[123]

A science that has not legitimated itself is not a true science; if
the discourse that was meant to legitimate it seems to belong to a
prescientific form of knowledge, like a "vulgar" narrative, it is de-
moted to the lowest rank, that of an ideology or instrument of
power. And this always happens if the rules of the science game that
discourse denounces as empirical are applied to science itself.

Take for example the speculative statement: "A scientific statement is knowledge if and only if it can take its place in a universal
process of engendering." The question is: Is this statement knowledge
as it itself defines it? Only if it can take its place in a universal process
of engendering. Which it can. All it has to do is to presuppose that
such a process exists (the Life of spirit) and that it is itself an expression of that process. This presupposition, in fact, is indispensable to
the speculative language game. Without it, the language of legitimation would not be legitimate; it would accompany science in a

nosedive into nonsense, at least if we take idealism's word for it.

But this presupposition can also be understood in a totally different sense, one which takes us in the direction of postmodern culture: we could say, in keeping with the perspective we adopted earlier, that this presupposition defines the set of rules one must accept in order to play the speculative game.[124] Such an appraisal assumes first that we accept that the "positive" sciences represent the general mode of knowledge and second, that we understand this language to imply certain formal and axiomatic presuppositions that it must always make explicit. This is exactly what Nietzsche is doing, though with a different terminology, when he shows that "European nihilism" resulted from the truth requirement of science being turned back against itself.[125]

There thus arises an idea of perspective that is not far removed, at least in this respect, from the idea of language games. What we have here is a process of delegitimation fueled by the demand for legitimation itself. The "crisis" of scientific knowledge, signs of which have been accumulating since the end of the nineteenth century, is not born of a chance proliferation of sciences, itself an effect of progress in technology and the expansion of capitalism. It represents, rather, an internal erosion of the legitimacy principle of knowledge. There is erosion at work inside the speculative game, and by loosening the weave of the encyclopedic net in which each science was to find its place, it eventually sets them free.

The classical dividing lines between the various fields of science are thus called into question—disciplines disappear, overlappings occur at the borders between sciences, and from these new territories are born. The speculative hierarchy of learning gives way to an immanent and, as it were, "flat" network of areas of inquiry, the respective frontiers of which are in constant flux. The old "faculties" splinter into institutes and foundations of all kinds, and the universities lose their function of speculative legitimation. Stripped of the responsibility for research (which was stifled by the speculative narrative), they limit themselves to the transmission of what is judged to be established knowledge, and through didactics they guarantee the replication of teachers rather than the production of researchers. This is the state in which Nietzsche finds and condemns them.[126]

The potential for erosion intrinsic to the other legitimation procedure, the emancipation apparatus flowing from the *Aufklärung,* is no less extensive than the one at work within speculative discourse. But it touches a different aspect. Its distinguishing characteristic is that it grounds the legitimation of science and truth in the autonomy of interlocutors involved in ethical, social, and political praxis. As we have seen, there are immediate problems with this form of legitimation: the difference between a denotative statement with cognitive value and a prescriptive statement with practical value is one of relevance, therefore of competence. There is nothing to prove that if a statement describing a real situation is true, it follows that a prescriptive statement-based upon it (the effect of which will necessarily be a modification of that reality) will be just.

Take, for example, a closed door. Between "The door is closed" and "Open the door" there is no relation of consequence as defined in propositional logic. The two statements belong to two autonomous sets of rules defining different kinds of relevance, and therefore of competence. Here, the effect of dividing reason into cognitive or theoretical reason on the one hand, and practical reason on the other, is to attack the legitimacy of the discourse of science. Not directly, but indirectly, by revealing that it is a language game with its own rules (of which the a priori conditions of knowledge in Kant provide a first glimpse) and that it has no special calling to supervise the game of praxis (nor the game of aesthetics, for that matter). The game of science is thus put on a par with the others.

If this "delegitimation" is pursued in the slightest and if its scope is widened (as Wittgenstein does in his own way, and thinkers such as Martin Buber and Emmanuel Lévinas in theirs)[127] the road is then open for an important current of postmodernity: science plays its own game; it is incapable of legitimating the other language games. The game of prescription, for example, escapes it. But above all, it is incapable of legitimating itself, as speculation assumed it could.

The social subject itself seems to dissolve in this dissemination of language games. The social bond is linguistic, but is not woven with a single thread. It is a fabric formed by the intersection of at least two (and in reality an indeterminate number) of language games, obeying different rules. Wittgenstein writes: "Our language can be seen as an ancient city: a maze of little streets and squares, of old and new houses, and of houses with additions from various periods; and this surrounded by a multitude of new boroughs with straight regular streets and uniform houses."[128] And to drive home that the principle of unitotality—or synthesis under the authority of a meta-discourse of knowledge—is inapplicable, he subjects the "town" of language to the old sorites paradox by asking: "how many houses or streets does it take before a town begins to be a town?"[129]

New languages are added to the old ones, forming suburbs of the old town: "the symbolism of chemistry and the notation of the infin-itesimal calculus."[130] Thirty-five years later we can add to the list: machine languages, the matrices of game theory, new systems of musical notation, systems of notation for nondenotative forms of logic (temporal logics, deontic logics, modal logics), the language of the genetic code, graphs of phonological structures, and so on.

We may form a pessimistic impression of this splintering: nobody speaks all of those languages, they have no universal metalanguage, the project of the system-subject is a failure, the goal of emancipa-tion has nothing to do with science, we are all stuck in the positivism of this or that discipline of learning, the learned scholars have turned into scientists, the diminished tasks of research have become compart-mentalized and no one can master them all.[131] Speculative or human-istic philosophy is forced to relinquish its legitimation duties,[132] which explains why philosophy is facing a crisis wherever it persists in arrogating such functions and is reduced to the study of systems of logic or the history of ideas where it has been realistic enough to surrender them.[133]

Turn-of-the-century Vienna was weaned on this pessimism: not just artists such as Musil, Kraus, Hofmannsthal, Loos, Schönberg, and Broch, but also the philosophers Mach and Wittgenstein.[134] They carried awareness of and theoretical and artistic responsibility for delegitimation as far as it could be taken. We can say today that the mourning process has been completed. There is no need to start all over again. Wittgenstein's strength is that he did not opt for the positivism that was being developed by the Vienna Circle,[135] but out-lined in his investigation of language games a kind of legitimation not based on performativity. That is what the postmodern world is all about. Most people have lost the nostalgia for the lost narrative. It in no way follows that they are reduced to barbarity. What saves them from it is their knowledge that legitimation can only spring from their own linguistic practice and communicational interaction. Science "smiling into its beard" at every other belief has taught them the harsh austerity of realism.[136]

11. Research and Its Legitimation through Performativity

Let us return to science and begin by examining the pragmatics of research. Its essential mechanisms are presently undergoing two important changes: a multiplication in methods of argumentation and a rising complexity level in the process of establishing proof.

Aristotle, Descartes, and John Stuart Mill, among others, attempted to lay down the rules governing how a denotative utterance can obtain its addressee's assent.[137] Scientific research sets no great store by these methods. As already stated, it can and does use methods the demonstrative properties of which seem to challenge classical reason. Bachelard compiled a list of them, and it is already incomplete.[138]

These languages are not employed haphazardly, however. Their use is subject to a condition we could call pragmatic: each must formulate its own rules and petition the addressee to accept them. To satisfy this condition, an axiomatic is defined that includes a definition of symbols to be used in the proposed language, a description of the form expressions in the language must take in order to gain acceptance (well-formed expressions), and an enumeration of the operations that may be performed on the accepted expressions (axioms in the narrow sense).[139]

But how do we know what an axiomatic should, or does in fact, contain? The conditions listed above are formal conditions. There has to be a metalanguage to determine whether a given language satisfies the formal conditions of an axiomatic; that metalanguage is logic.

At this point a brief clarification is necessary. The alternative between someone who begins by establishing an axiomatic and then uses it to produce what are defined as acceptable statements, and a scientist who begins by establishing and stating facts and then tries to discover the axiomatics of the language he used in making his statements, is not a logical alternative, but only an empirical one. It is certainly of great importance for the researcher, and also for the philosopher, but in each case the question of the validation of statements is the same.[140]

The following question is more pertinent to legitimation: By what criteria does the logician define the properties required of an axiomatic? Is there a model for scientific languages? If so, is there just one? Is it verifiable? The properties generally required of the syntax of a formal system[141] are consistency (for example, a system inconsistent with respect to negation would admit both a proposition and its opposite), syntactic completeness (the system would lose its consistency if an axiom were added to it), decidability (there must be an effective procedure for deciding whether a given proposition belongs to the system or not), and the independence of the axioms in relation to one another. Now Gödel has effectively established the existence in the arithmetic system of a proposition that is neither demonstrable nor refutable within that system; this entails that the arithmetic system fails to satisfy the condition of completeness.[142]

Since it is possible to generalize this situation, it must be accepted that all formal systems have internal limitations.[143] This applies to logic: the metalanguage it uses to describe an artificial (axiomatic) language is "natural" or "everyday" language; that language is universal, since all other languages can be translated into it, but it is not consistent with respect to negation—it allows the formation of paradoxes.[144]

This necessitates a reformulation of the question of the legitimation of knowledge. When a denotative statement is declared true, there is a presupposition that the axiomatic system within which it is decidable and demonstrable has already been formulated, that it is known to the interlocutors, and that they have accepted that it is as formally satisfactory as possible. This was the spirit in which the mathematics of the Bourbaki group was developed.[145] But analogous observations can be made for the other sciences: they owe their status to the existence of a language whose rules of functioning cannot themselves be demonstrated but are the object of a consensus among experts. These rules, or at least some of them, are requests. The request is a modality of prescription.

The argumentation required for a scientific statement to be accepted is thus subordinated to a "first" acceptance (which is in fact constantly renewed by virtue of the principle of recursion) of the rules defining the allowable means of argumentation. Two noteworthy properties of scientific knowledge result from this: the flexibility of its means, that is, the plurality of its languages; and its character as a pragmatic game—the acceptability of the "moves" (new propositions) made in it depends on a contract drawn between the partners. Another result is that there are two different kinds of "progress" in knowledge: one corresponds to a new move (a new argument) within the established rules; the other, to the invention of new rules, in other words, a change to a new game.[146]

Obviously, a major shift in the notion of reason accompanies this new arrangement. The principle of a universal metalanguage is replaced by the principle of a plurality of formal and axiomatic systems capable of arguing the truth of denotative statements; these systems are described by a metalanguage that is universal but not consistent. What used to pass as paradox, and even paralogism, in the knowledge of classical and modern science can, in certain of these systems, acquire a new force of conviction and win the acceptance of the community of experts.[147] The language game method I have followed here can claim a modest place in this current of thought.

The other fundamental aspect of research, the production of proof, takes us in quite a different direction. It is in principle part of an argumentation process designed to win acceptance for a new statement (for example, giving testimony or presenting an exhibit in the case of judicial rhetoric).[148] But it presents a special problem: it is here that the referent ("reality") is called to the stand and cited in the debate between scientists.

I have already made the point that the question of proof is problematical since proof needs to be proven. One can begin by publishing a description of how the proof was obtained, so other scientists can check the result by repeating the same process. But the fact still has to be observed in order to stand proven. What constitutes a scientific observation? A fact that has been registered by an eye, an ear, a sense organ?[149] Senses are deceptive, and their range and powers of discrimination are limited.

This is where technology comes in. Technical devices originated as prosthetic aids for the human organs or as physiological systems whose function it is to receive data or condition the context.[150] They follow a principle, and it is the principle of optimal performance: maximizing output (the information or modifications obtained) and minimizing input (the energy expended in the process).[151] Technology is therefore a game pertaining not to the true, the just, or the beautiful, etc., but to efficiency: a technical "move" is "good" when it does better and/or expends less energy than another.

This definition of technical competence is a late development. For a long time inventions came in fits and starts, the products of chance research, or research as much or more concerned with the arts (*technai*) than with knowledge: the Greeks of the Classical period, for example, established no close relationship between knowledge and technology.[152] In the sixteenth and seventeenth centuries, the work of "perspectors" was still a matter of curiosity and artistic innovation.[153] This was the case until the end of the eighteenth century.[154] And it can be maintained that even today "wildcat" activities of technical invention, sometimes related to *bricolage*, still go on outside the imperatives of scientific argumentation.[155]

Nonetheless, the need for proof becomes increasingly strong as the pragmatics of scientific knowledge replaces traditional knowledge or knowledge based on revelation. By the end of the *Discourse on Method*, Descartes is already asking for laboratory funds. A new problem appears: devices that optimize the performance of the human body for the purpose of producing proof require additional expenditures. No money, no proof—and that means no verification of statements and no truth. The games of scientific language become the games of the rich, in which whoever is wealthiest has the best chance of being right. An equation between wealth, efficiency, and truth is thus established.

What happened at the end of the eighteenth century, with the first industrial revolution, is that the reciprocal of this equation was discovered: no technology without wealth, but no wealth without technology. A technical apparatus requires an investment; but since it optimizes the efficiency of the task to which it is applied, it also optimizes the surplus-value derived from this improved performance. All that is needed is for the surplus-value to be realized, in other words, for the product of the task performed to be sold. And the system can be sealed in the following way: a portion of the sale is recycled into a research fund dedicated to further performance improvement. It is at this precise moment that science becomes a force of production, in other words, a moment in the circulation of capital.

It was more the desire for wealth than the desire for knowledge that initially forced upon technology the imperative of performance improvement and product realization. The "organic" connection between technology and profit preceded its union with science. Technology became important to contemporary knowledge only through the mediation of a generalized spirit of performativity. Even today, progress in knowledge is not totally subordinated to technological investment.[156]

Capitalism solves the scientific problem of research funding in its own way: directly by financing research departments in private companies, in which demands for performativity and recommercialization orient research first and foremost toward technological "applications"; and indirectly by creating private, state, or mixed-sector research foundations that grant program subsidies to university departments, research laboratories, and independent research groups with no expectation of an immediate return on the results of the work—this is done on the theory that research must be financed at a loss for certain length of time in order to increase the probability of its yielding a decisive, and therefore highly profitable, innovation.[157] Nation-states, especially in their Keynesian period, follow the same rule: applied research on the one hand, basic research on the other. They collaborate with corporations through an array of agencies.[158] The prevailing corporate norms of work management spread to the applied science laboratories: hierarchy, centralized decision making, teamwork, calculation of individual and collective returns, the development of saleable programs, market research, and so on.[159] Centers dedicated to "pure" research suffer from this less, but also receive less funding.

The production of proof, which is in principle only part of an argumentation process designed to win agreement from the addressees of scientific messages, thus falls under the control of another language game, in which the goal is no longer truth, but performativity—that is, the best possible input/output equation. The State and/or company must abandon the idealist and humanist narratives of legitimation in order to justify the new goal: in the discourse of today's financial backers of research, the only credible goal is power. Scientists, technicians, and instruments are purchased not to find truth, but to augment power.

The question is to determine what the discourse of power consists of and if it can constitute a legitimation. At first glance, it is prevented from doing so by the traditional distinction between force and right, between force and wisdom—in other words, between what is strong, what is just, and what is true. I referred to this incommensurability earlier in terms of the theory of language games, when I distinguished the denotative game (in which what is relevant is the true/false distinction) from the prescriptive game (in which the just/unjust distinction pertains) from the technical game (in which the criterion is the efficient/inefficient distinction). "Force" appears to belong exclusively to the last game, the game of technology. I am excluding the case in which force operates by means of terror. This lies outside the realm of language games, because the efficacy of such force is based entirely on the threat to eliminate the opposing player, not on making a better "move" than he. Whenever efficiency (that is, obtaining the desired effect) is derived from a "Say or do this, or else you'll never speak again," then we are in the realm of terror, and the social bond is destroyed.

But the fact remains that since performativity increases the ability to produce proof, it also increases the ability to be right: the technical criterion, introduced on a massive scale into scientific knowledge, cannot fail to influence the truth criterion. The same has been said of the relationship between justice and performance: the probability that an order would be pronounced just was said to increase with its chances of being implemented, which would in turn increase with the performance capability of the prescriber. This led Luhmann to hypothesize that in postindustrial societies the normativity of laws is replaced by the performativity of procedures.[160] "Context control," in other words, performance improvement won at the expense of the partner or partners constituting that context (be they "nature" or men), can pass for a kind of legitimation.[161] De facto legitimation.

This procedure operates within the following framework: since "reality" is what provides the evidence used as proof in scientific argumentation, and also provides prescriptions and promises of a juridical, ethical, and political nature with results, one can master all of these games by mastering "reality." That is precisely what technology can do. By reinforcing technology, one "reinforces" reality, and one's chances of being just and right increase accordingly. Reciprocally, technology is reinforced all the more effectively if one has access to scientific knowledge and decision-making authority.

This is how legitimation by power takes shape. Power is not only good performativity, but also effective verification and good verdicts. It legitimates science and the law on the basis of their efficiency, and legitimates this efficiency on the basis of science and law. It is self-legitimating, in the same way a system organized around performance maximization seems to be.[162] Now it is precisely this kind of context control that a generalized computerization of society may bring. The performativity of an utterance, be it denotative or prescriptive, increases proportionally to the amount of information about its referent one has at one's disposal. Thus the growth of power, and its self-legitimation, are now taking the route of data storage and accessibility, and the operativity of information.

The relationship between science and technology is reversed. The complexity of the argumentation becomes relevant here, especially because it necessitates greater sophistication in the means of obtaining proof, and that in turn benefits performativity. Research funds are allocated by States, corporations, and nationalized companies in accordance with this logic of power growth. Research sectors that are unable to argue that they contribute even indirectly to the optimization of the system's performance are abandoned by the flow of capital and doomed to senescence. The criterion of performance is explicitly invoked by the authorities to justify their refusal to subsidize certain research centers.[163]

12. Education and Its Legitimation through Performativity

It should be easy to describe how the other facet of knowledge—its transmission, or education—is affected by the predominance of the performativity criterion.

If we accept the notion that there is an established body of knowledge, the question of its transmission, from a pragmatic point of view, can be subdivided into a series of questions: Who transmits learning? What is transmitted? To whom? Through what medium? In what form? With what effect?[164] A university policy is formed by a coherent set of answers to these questions.

If the performativity of the supposed social system is taken as the criterion of relevance (that is, when the perspective of systems theory is adopted), higher education becomes a subsystem of the social system, and the same performativity criterion is applied to each of these problems.

The desired goal becomes the optimal contribution of higher education to the best performativity of the social system. Accordingly, it will have to create the skills that are indispensable to that system. These are of two kinds. The first kind are more specifically designed to tackle world competition. They vary according to which "specialities" the nation-states or major educational institutions can sell on the world market. If our general hypothesis is correct, there will be a growth in demand for experts and high and middle management executives in the leading sectors mentioned at the beginning of this study, which is where the action will be in the years to come: any discipline with applicability to training in "telematics" (computer scientists, cyberneticists, linguists, mathematicians, logicians . . .) will most likely receive priority in education. All the more so since an increase in the number of these experts should speed the research in other learning sectors, as has been the case with medicine and biology.

Secondly, and still within the same general hypothesis, higher learning will have to continue to supply the social system with the skills fulfilling society's own needs, which center on maintaining its internal cohesion. Previously, this task entailed the formation and dissemination of a general model of life, most often legitimated by the emancipation narrative. In the context of delegitimation, universities and the institutions of higher learning are called upon to create skills, and no longer ideals—so many doctors, so many teachers in a given discipline, so many engineers, so many administrators, etc. The transmission of knowledge is no longer designed to train an elite capable of guiding the nation towards its emancipation, but to supply the system with players capable of acceptably fulfilling their roles at the pragmatic posts required by its institutions.[165]

If the ends of higher learning are functional, what of its addressees? The student has changed already and will certainly change more. He is no longer a youth from the "liberal elite,"[166] more or less concerned with the great task of social progress, understood in terms of emancipation. In this sense, the "democratic" university (no entrance requirements, little cost to the student and even to society if the price per student is calculated, high enrollment),[167] which was modeled along the principles of emancipationist humanism, today seems to offer little in the way of performance.[168] Higher education is in fact already undergoing a major realignment, dictated both by administrative measures and by social demands (themselves rather uncontrolled) emanating from the new users; the tendency is to divide the functions of higher learning into two broad categories of services.

In its function of professional training, higher education still addresses itself to the young of the liberal elite, to whom it transmits the competence judged necessary by each profession. They are joined through one route or another (for example, institutes of technology) —all of which, however, conform to the same didactic model—by the addressees of the new domains of knowledge linked to the new techniques and technologies. They are, once again, young people who have yet to become "active."

Aside from these two categories of students, who reproduce the "professional intelligentsia" and the "technical intelligentsia,"[169] the remainder of the young people present in the universities are for the most part unemployed who are not counted as job seekers in the statistics, though they outnumber the openings in their disciplines arts and human sciences). Despite their age, they do in fact belong to the new category of the addressees of knowledge.

For in addition to its professionalist function, the University is beginning, or should begin, to play a new role in improving the system's performance—that of job retraining and continuing education.[170] Outside the universities, departments, or institutions with a professional orientation, knowledge will no longer be transmitted *en bloc,* once and for all, to young people before their entry into the work force: rather it is and will be served "à la carte" to adults who are either already working or expect to be, for the purpose of improving their skills and chances of promotion, but also to help them acquire information, languages, and language games allowing them both to widen their occupational horizons and to articulate their technical and ethical experience.[171]

The new course that the transmission of knowledge is taking is not without conflict. As much as it is in the interests of the system, and therefore of its "decision makers," to encourage professional advancement (since it can only improve the performance of the whole), any experimentation in discourse, institutions, and values (with the inevitable "disorders" it brings in the curriculum, student supervision and testing, and pedagogy—not to mention its socio-political repercussions) is regarded as having little or no operational value and is not given the slightest credence in the name of the seriousness of the system. Such experimentation offers an escape from functionalism; it should not be dismissed lightly since it was functionalism itself that pointed the way.[172] But it is safe to assume that responsibility for it will devolve upon extrauniversity networks.[173]

In any case, even if the performativity principle does not always help pinpoint the policy to follow, its general effect is to subordinate the institutions of higher learning to the existing powers. The moment knowledge ceases to be an end in itself—the realization of the Idea or the emancipation of men—its transmission is no longer the exclusive responsibility of scholars and students. The notion of "university franchise" now belongs to a bygone era. The "autonomy" granted the universities after the crisis of the late 1960s has very little meaning given the fact that practically nowhere do teachers' groups have the power to decide what the budget of their institution will be;[174] all they can do is allocate the funds that are assigned to them, and only then as the last step in the process.[175]

What is transmitted in higher learning? In the case of professional training, and limiting ourselves to a narrowly functionalist point of view, an organized stock of established knowledge is the essential thing that is transmitted. The application of new technologies to this stock may have a considerable impact on the medium of communication. It does not seem absolutely necessary that the medium be a lecture delivered in person by a teacher in front of silent students, with questions reserved for sections or "practical work" sessions run by an assistant. To the extent that learning is translatable into computer language and the traditional teacher is replaceable by memory banks, didactics can be entrusted to machines linking traditional memory banks (libraries, etc.) and computer data banks to intelligent terminals placed at the students' disposal.

Pedagogy would not necessarily suffer. The students would still have to be taught something: not contents, but how to use the terminals. On the one hand, that means teaching new languages and on the other, a more refined ability to handle the language game of interrogation—where should the question be addressed, in other words, what is the relevant memory bank for what needs to be known? How should the question be formulated to avoid misunderstandings? etc.[176] From this point of view, elementary training in informatics, and especially telematics, should be a basic requirement in universities, in the same way that fluency in a foreign language is now, for example.[177]

It is only in the context of the grand narratives of legitimation — the life of the spirit and/or the emancipation of humanity — that the partial replacement of teachers by machines may seem inadequate or even intolerable. But it is probable that these narratives are already no longer the principal driving force behind interest in acquiring knowledge. If the motivation is power, then this aspect of classical didactics ceases to be relevant. The question (overt or implied) now asked by the professionalist student, the State, or institutions of higher education is no longer "Is it true?" but "What use is it?" In the context of the mercantilization of knowledge, more often than not this question is equivalent to: "Is it saleable?" And in the context of power-growth: "Is it efficient?" Having competence in a performance-oriented skill does indeed seem saleable in the conditions described above, and it is efficient by definition. What no longer makes the grade is competence as defined by other criteria true/false, just/unjust, etc. — and, of course, low performativity in general.

This creates the prospect for a vast market for competence in operational skills. Those who possess this kind of knowledge will be the object of offers or even seduction policies.[178] Seen in this light, what we are approaching is not the end of knowledge — quite the contrary. Data banks are the Encyclopedia of tomorrow. They transcend the capacity of each of their users. They are "nature" for postmodern man.[179]

It should be noted, however, that didactics does not simply consist in the transmission of information; and competence, even when defined as a performance skill, does not simply reduce to having a good memory for data or having easy access to a computer. It is a commonplace that what is of utmost importance is the capacity to actualize the relevant data for solving a problem "here and now," and to organize that data into an efficient strategy.

As long as the game is not a game of perfect information, the advantage will be with the player who has knowledge and can obtain information. By definition, this is the case with a student in a learning situation. But in games of perfect information,[180] the best performativity cannot consist in obtaining additional information in this way. It comes rather from arranging the data in a new way, which is what constitutes a "move" properly speaking. This new arrangement is usually achieved by connecting together series of data that were previously held to be independent.[181] This capacity to articulate what used to be separate can be called imagination. Speed is one of its properties.[182] It is possible to conceive the world of postmodern knowledge as governed by a game of perfect information, in the sense that the data is in principle accessible to any expert: there is no scientific secret. Given equal competence (no longer in the acquisition of knowledge, but in its production), what extra performativity depends on in the final analysis is "imagination," which allows one either to make a new move or change the rules of the game.

If education must not only provide for the reproduction of skills, but also for their progress, then it follows that the transmission of knowledge should not be limited to the transmission of information, but should include training in all of the procedures that can increase one's ability to connect the fields jealously guarded from one another by the traditional organization of knowledge. The slogan of "interdisciplinary studies," which became particularly popular after the crisis of 1968 but was being advocated long before that, seems to move in this direction. It ran up against the feudalism of the universities, they say. It ran up against more than that.

In Humboldt's model of the University, each science has its own place in a system crowned by speculation. Any encroachment of one science into another's field can only create confusion, "noise" in the system. Collaboration can only take place on the level of speculation, in the heads of the philosophers.

The idea of an interdisciplinary approach is specific to the age of delegitimation and its hurried empiricism. The relation to knowledge is not articulated in terms of the realization of the life of the spirit or the emancipation of humanity, but in terms of the users of a complex conceptual and material machinery and those who benefit from its performance capabilities. They have at their disposal no metalanguage or metanarrative in which to formulate the final goal and correct use of that machinery. But they do have brainstorming to improve its performance.

The emphasis placed on teamwork is related to the predominance of the performativity criterion in knowledge. When it comes to speaking the truth or prescribing justice, numbers are meaningless. They only make a difference if justice and truth are thought of in terms of the probability of success. In general, teamwork does in fact improve performance, if it is done under certain conditions detailed long ago by social scientists.[183] In particular, it has been established that teamwork is especially successful in improving performativity within the framework of a given model, that is, for the implementation of a task. Its advantages seem less certain when the need is to "imagine" new models, in other words, on the level of their conception. There have apparently been cases where even this has worked,[184] but it is difficult to isolate what is attributable to the team setup and what derived from the individual talent of the team members.

It will be observed that this orientation is concerned more with the production of knowledge (research) than its transmission. To separate them completely is to fall into abstraction and is probably counterproductive even within the framework of functionalism and professionalism. And yet the solution toward which the institutions of knowledge all over the world are in fact moving consists in dissociating these two aspects of didactics—"simple" reproduction and "extended" reproduction. This is being done by earmarking entities of all kinds—institutions, levels or programs within institutions, groupings of institutions, groupings of disciplines—either for the selection and reproduction of professional skills, or for the promotion and "stimulation" of "imaginative" minds. The transmission channels to which the first category is given access can be simplified and made available on a mass scale. the second category has the privilege of working on a smaller scale in conditions of aristocratic egalitarianism.[185] It matters little whether the latter are officially a part of the universities.

But one thing that seems certain is that in both cases the process of delegitimation and the predominance of the performance criterion are sounding the knell of the age of the Professor: a professor is no more competent than memory bank networks in transmitting established knowledge, no more competent than interdisciplinary teams in imagining new moves or new games.

13. Postmodern Science as the Search for Instabilities

As previously indicated, the pragmatics of scientific research, especially in its search for new methods of argumentation, emphasizes the invention of new "moves" and even new rules for language games. We must now take a closer look at this aspect of the problem, which is of decisive importance in the present state of scientific knowledge. We could say, tongue in cheek, that scientific knowledge is seeking a "crisis resolution"—a resolution of the crisis of determinism. Determinism is the hypothesis upon which legitimation by performativity is based: since performativity is defined by an input/ output ratio, there is a presupposition that the system into which the input is entered is stable; that system must follow a regular "path" that it is possible to express as a continuous function possessing a derivative, so that an accurate prediction of the output can be made.

Such is the positivist "philosophy" of efficiency. I will cite a number of prominent examples as evidence against it to facilitate the final discussion of legitimation. Briefly, the aim is to demonstrate on the basis of a few exhibits that the pragmatics of postmodern scientific knowledge per se has little affinity with the quest for performativity.

Science does not expand by means of the positivism of efficiency. The opposite is true: working on a proof means searching for and "in- venting" counterexamples, in other words, the unintelligible; sup- porting an argument means looking for a "paradox" and legitimating it with new rules in the games of reasoning. In neither case is effi- ciency sought for its own sake; it comes, sometimes tardily, as an extra, when the grant givers finally decide to take an interest in the case.[186] But what never fails to come and come again, with every new theory, new hypothesis, new statement, or new observation, is the question of legitimacy. For it is not philosophy that asks this question of science, but science that asks it of itself.

What is outdated is not asking what is true and what is just, but viewing science as positivistic, relegating it to the status of unlegiti- mated learning, half-knowledge, as did the German idealists. The question, "What is your argument worth, what is your proof worth?" is so much a part of the pragmatics of scientific knowledge that it is what assures the transformation of the addressee of a given argument and proof into the sender of a new argument and proof—thereby assuring the renewal of scientific discourse and the replacement of each generation of scientists. Science develops—and no one will deny that it develops—by developing this question. And this question, as it develops, leads to the following question, that is to say, metaques- tion, the question of legitimacy: "What is your 'what is it worth' worth?"[187]

I made the point that the striking feature of postmodern scientific knowledge is that the discourse on the rules that validate it is (ex- plicitly) immanent to it.[188] What was considered at the end of the nineteenth century to be a loss of legitimacy and a fall into philo- sophical "pragmatism" or logical positivism was only an episode, from which knowledge has recovered by including within scientific discourse the discourse on the validation of statements held to be laws. As we have seen, this inclusion is not a simple operation, but gives rise to "paradoxes" that are taken extremely seriously and to "limitations" on the scope of knowledge that are in fact changes in its nature.

The metamathematical research that led to Gödel's theorem is a veritable paradigm of how this change in nature takes place.[189] But the transformation that dynamics has undergone is no less exemplary of the new scientific spirit, and it is of particular interest here because it compels us to reconsider a notion that, as we have seen, figures prominently in the discussion of performance, particularly in the domain of social theory: the notion of system.

The idea of performance implies a highly stable system because it is based on the principle of a relation, which is in theory always calculable, between heat and work, hot source and cold source, input and output. This idea comes from thermodynamics. It is associated with the notion that the evolution of a system's performance can be predicated if all of the variables are known. The ideal fulfillment of this condition is clearly expressed in Laplace's fiction of the "demon:"[190] he knows all of the variables determining the state of the universe at a moment t, and can thus predict its state at a moment $t'>t$. This fiction is sustained by the principle that physical systems, including the system of systems called the universe, follow regular patterns, with the result that their evolution traces a regular path and gives rise to "normal" continuous functions (and to futurology . . .).

The advent of quantum mechanics and atomic physics has limited the range of applicability of this principle in two ways, the respective implications of which differ in scope. First, a complete definition of the initial state of a system (or all the independent variables) would require an expenditure of energy at least equivalent to that consumed by the system to be defined. A layman's version of the de facto impossibility of ever achieving a complete measure of any given state of a system is provided in a note by Borges. An emperor wishes to have a perfectly accurate map of the empire made. The project leads the country to ruin—the entire population devotes all its energy to cartography.[191]

Brillouin's argument[192] leads to the conclusion that the idea (or ideology) of perfect control over a system, which is supposed to improve its performance, is inconsistent with respect to the law of contradiction: it in fact lowers the performance level it claims to raise. This inconsistency explains the weakness of state and socioeconomic bureaucracies: they stifle the systems or subsystems they control and asphyxiate themselves in the process (negative feedback). The interest of such an explanation is that it has no need to invoke any form of legitimation outside the system itself (for example, the freedom of human agents inciting them to rise up against excessive authority). Even if we accept that society is a system, complete control over it, which would necessitate an exact definition of its initial state, is impossible because no such definition could ever be effected.

But this limitation only calls into question the practicability of exact knowledge and the power that would result from it. They remain possible in theory. Classical determinism continues to work within the framework of the unreachable—but conceivable—limit of the total knowledge of a system.[193]

Quantum theory and microphysics require a far more radical revision of the idea of a continuous and predictable path. The quest for precision is not limited by its cost, but by the very nature of matter. It is not true that uncertainty (lack of control) decreases as accuracy goes up: it goes up as well. Jean Perrin offers as an example of this the measurement of the real density (the mass/volume quotient) of a given quantity of air contained in a sphere. It varies noticeably when the volume of the sphere is reduced from 100 m^3 to 1 cm^3; there is very little variation when it is reduced from 1 cm^3 to $1/1000 \text{ mm}^3$, although already in this range irregularly occurring variations of the order of a billionth can be observed. As the volume of the sphere decreases, the size of the variations increases: for a volume of 1/10th of a cubic micron, the variations are of the order of a thousandth; and for 1/100th of a cubic micron, they are of the order of 1/5th.

Further decreasing the volume brings us to the molecular scale. If the spherule is located in the void between two molecules of air, the real density of the air in it is nil. But about one time in a thousand, the center of the spherule will "fall" within a molecule, and the average density is then comparable to what is called the real density of the gas. Reduced to intra-atomic dimensions, chances are high that it will be located in the void, once again with a density of zero. But one time in a million its center will fall within a corpuscle or in the nucleus of the atom, and when it does the density will be several million times greater than that of water. "If the spherule contracts still further . . . the average density and the real density will probably soon become nil and remain nil, except in some very rare positions where it will reach values spectacularly higher than those obtained previously."[194]

Knowledge about the density of air thus resolves into a multiplicity of absolutely incompatible statements; they can only be made compatible if they are relativized in relation to a scale chosen by the speaker. In addition, on certain levels, the statement of density cannot be made in the form of a simple assertion, but only as a modalized assertion of the type: it is plausible that the density will be equal to zero but not out of the question that it will be of the order of 10^n, where n is a very large number.

Here, the relation between the scientist's statement and "what 'nature' says" seems to be organized as a game without perfect information. The modalization of the scientist's statement reflects the fact that the effective, singular statement (the token) that nature will produce is unpredictable. All that can be calculated is the probability that the statement will say one thing rather than another. On the level of microphysics, "better" information—in other words, information with a higher performance capability—cannot be obtained. The problem is not to learn what the opponent ("nature") is, but to identify the game it plays. Einstein balked at the idea that "God plays with dice."[195] Yet dice is precisely a game for which this kind of "sufficient" statistical regularities can be established (so much for the old image of the supreme Determinant). If God played bridge, then the level of "primary chance" encountered by science could no longer be imputed to the indifference of the die toward which face is up, but would have to be attributed to cunning—in other words, to a choice, itself left up to chance, between a number of possible, pure strategies.[196]

It is generally accepted that nature is an indifferent, not deceptive, opponent, and it is upon this basis that the distinction is made between the natural and the human sciences.[197] In pragmatic terms, this means that in the natural sciences "nature" is the referent—mute, but as predictable as a die thrown a great number of times—about which scientists exchange denotative utterances constituting moves they play against one another. In the human sciences, on the other hand, the referent (man) is a participant in the game, one that speaks and develops a strategy (a mixed strategy, perhaps) to counter that of the scientist: here, the kind of chance with which the scientist is confronted is not object based or indifferent, but behavioral or strategic[198] —in other words, agonistic.

It will be argued that these problems concern microphysics and that they do not prevent the establishment of continuous functions exact enough to form the basis of probabilistic predictions for the evolution of a given system. This is the reasoning systems theorists—

who are also the theorists of legitimation by performance—use to try to regain their rights. There is, however, a current in contemporary mathematics that questions the very possibility of precise measurement and thus the prediction of the behavior of objects even on the human scale.

Mandelbrot cites as a source the text by Perrin discussed above. But he extends the analysis in an unexpected direction. "The functions with derivatives," he writes, "are the simplest and easiest to work with, they are nevertheless exceptional. Using geometrical language, curves that have no tangent are the rule, and regular curves, such as the circle, are interesting, but quite special."[199]

This observation is not just an object for idle curiosity but is valid for most experimental data: the contours of a floccule of soapy, salinated water present such irregularities that it is impossible for the eye to draw a tangent to any point on its surface. The applicable model here is that of Brownian movement, a well-known property of which is that the vector of the particle's movement from a given point is isotropic, in other words, all possible directions are equally probable.

But we run into the same problem on more familiar levels as well—if, for example, we wish to make a precise measurement of the coast of Brittany, the crater-filled surface of the moon, the distribution of stellar matter, the frequency of bursts of interference during a telephone call, turbulence in general, the shape of clouds. In short, the majority of the objects whose outlines and distributions have not undergone regularization at the hands of man.

Mandelbrot shows that data of this kind describe curves similar to those of continuous functions for which no derivative exists. A simplified model of this is Koch's curve;[200] it is self-similar, and it can be shown that the dimension of self-similarity in which it is constructed is not a whole number but log 4/log 3. It would be justified to say of such a curve that it is located in a space whose "number of dimensions" is between one and two, and thus that it lies intuitively somewhere between a line and a flat surface. Because their relevant dimension of self-similarity is a fraction, Mandelbrot calls objects of this kind fractals.

The work of René Thom moves in a similar direction.[201] He directly questions the validity of the notion of a stable system, which is a presupposition in Laplace's determinism and even in probability theory.

Thom constructs a mathematical language allowing a formal description of the discontinuities that can occur in determined phenomena, causing them to take unexpected forms: this language constitutes what is known as catastrophe theory.

Take aggressiveness as a state variable of a dog: it increases in direct proportion to the dog's anger, a control variable.[202] Supposing the dog's anger is measurable, when it reaches a certain threshold it is expressed in the form of an attack. Fear, the second control variable, has the opposite effect; when it reaches its threshold it is expressed as flight. In the absence of anger or fear, the dog's behavior is stable (the top of Gauss's curve). But if the two control variables increase together, the two thresholds will be approached simultaneously: the dog's behavior becomes unpredictable and can switch abruptly from attack to flight, and vice versa. The system is said to be unstable: the control variables are continuous, but the state variables are discontinuous.

Thom shows that it is possible to write an equation expressing an instability of this kind and also to plot a graph (which is three dimensional, since there are two control variables and one state variable) mapping all of the movements of the point representing the dog's behavior, including the abrupt passage from one type of behavior to the other. The equation is characteristic of a class of catastrophes, which is defined by its number of control and state variables (here 2 + 1).

This provides us with an answer in the debate between stable and unstable systems, determinism and nondeterminism. Thom formulates it as a postulate: "The more or less determined character of a process is determined by the local state of the process."[203] Determinism is a type of functioning that is itself determined: in every case nature produces the least complex local morphology compatible with the initial local circumstances.[204] But it is possible—in fact, it is most frequently the case—that these circumstances will prevent the production of a stable form. This happens because the circumstances are usually in conflict: "The catastrophe model reduces all causative processes to a single one, easy to justify intuitively: conflict, the father of all things according to Heraclitus,"[205] It is more probable that the control variables will be incompatible than the opposite. All that exist are "islands of determinism." Catastrophic antagonism is literally the rule: there are rules for the general agonistics of series, determined by the number of variables in play.

It is not out of the question to establish an (admittedly weak) parallel between Thom's work and the research of the Palo Alto school, especially in its application of paradoxology to the study of schizophrenia, known as the Double Bind Theory.[206] Here, I will do no more than note the connection. The theory helps us understand how research centered on singularities and "incommensurabilities" is applicable to the pragmatics of the most everyday problems.

The conclusion we can draw from this research (and much more not mentioned here) is that the continuous differentiable function is losing its preeminence as a paradigm of knowledge and prediction. Postmodern science—by concerning itself with such things as undecidables, the limits of precise control, conflicts characterized by incomplete information, "*fracta*," catastrophes, and pragmatic paradoxes—is theorizing its own evolution as discontinuous, catastrophic, nonrectifiable, and paradoxical. It is changing the meaning of the word *knowledge,* while expressing how such a change can take place. It is producing not the known, but the unknown. And it suggests a model of legitimation that has nothing to do with maximized performance, but has as its basis difference understood as paralogy.[207]

A game theory specialist whose work is moving in this same direction said it well: "Wherein, then, does the usefulness of game theory lie? Game theory, we think, is useful in the same sense that any sophisticated theory is useful, namely as a generator of ideas."[208] P. B. Medawar, for his part, has stated that "*having ideas* is the scientist's highest accomplishment,"[209] that there is no "scientific method,"[210] and that a scientist is before anything else a person who "tells stories." The only difference is that he is duty bound to verify them.

14. Legitimation by Paralogy

Let us say at this point that the facts we have presented concerning the problem of the legitimation of knowledge today are sufficient for our purposes. We no longer have recourse to the grand narratives—we can resort neither to the dialectic of Spirit nor even to the emancipation of humanity as a validation for postmodern scientific discourse. But as we have just seen, the little narrative [*petit récit*] remains the quintessential form of imaginative invention, most particularly in science.[211] In addition, the principle of consensus as a criterion of validation seems to be inadequate. It has two formulations. In the first, consensus is an agreement between men, defined as knowing intellects and free wills, and is obtained through dialogue. This is the form elaborated by Habermas, but his conception is based on the validity of the narrative of emancipation. In the second, consensus is a component of the system, which manipulates it in order to maintain and improve its performance.[212] It is the object of administrative procedures, in Luhmann's sense. In this case, its only validity is as an instrument to be used toward achieving the real goal, which is what legitimates the system—power.

The problem is therefore to determine whether it is possible to have a form of legitimation based solely on paralogy. Paralogy must be distinguished from innovation: the latter is under the command of the system, or at least used by it to improve its efficiency; the former is a move (the importance of which is often not recognized until later) played in the pragmatics of knowledge. The fact that it is in reality frequently, but not necessarily, the case that one is transformed into the other presents no difficulties for the hypothesis.

Returning to the description of scientific pragmatics (section 7), it is now dissension that must be emphasized. Consensus is a horizon that is never reached. Research that takes place under the aegis of a paradigm[213] tends to stabilize; it is like the exploitation of a technological, economic, or artistic "idea." It cannot be discounted. But what is striking is that someone always comes along to disturb the order of "reason." It is necessary to posit the existence of a power that destabilizes the capacity for explanation, manifested in the promulgation of new norms for understanding or, if one prefers, in a proposal to establish new rules circumscribing a new field of research for the language of science. This, in the context of scientific discussion, is the same process Thom calls morphogenesis. It is not without rules (there are classes of catastrophes), but it is always locally determined. Applied to scientific discussion and placed in a temporal framework, this property implies that "discoveries" are unpredictable. In terms of the idea of transparency, it is a factor that generates blind spots and defers consensus.[214]

This summary makes it easy to see that systems theory and the kind of legitimation it proposes have no scientific basis whatsoever; science itself does not function according to this theory's paradigm of the system, and contemporary science excludes the possibility of using such a paradigm to describe society.

In this context, let us examine two important points in Luhmann's argument. On the one hand, the system can only function by reducing complexity, and on the other, it must induce the adaptation of individual aspirations to its own ends.[215] The reduction in complexity is required to maintain the system's power capability. If all messages could circulate freely among all individuals, the quantity of the information that would have to be taken into account before making the correct choice would delay decisions considerably, thereby lowering performativity. Speed, in effect, is a power component of the system.

The objection will be made that these molecular opinions must indeed be taken into account if the risk of serious disturbances is to be avoided. Luhmann replies—and this is the second point—that it is possible to guide individual aspirations through a process of "quasi-apprenticeship," "free of all disturbance," in order to make them compatible with the system's decisions. The decisions do not have to respect individuals' aspirations: the aspirations have to aspire to the decisions, or at least to their effects. Administrative procedures should make individuals "want" what the system needs in order to perform well.[216] It is easy to see what role telematics technology could play in this.

It cannot be denied that there is persuasive force in the idea that context control and domination are inherently better than their absence. The performativity criterion has its "advantages." It excludes in principle adherence to a metaphysical discourse; it requires the renunciation of fables; it demands clear minds and cold wills; it replaces the definition of essences with the calculation of interactions; it makes the "players" assume responsibility not only for the statements they propose, but also for the rules to which they submit those statements in order to render them acceptable. It brings the pragmatic functions of knowledge clearly to light, to the extent that they seem to relate to the criterion of efficiency: the pragmatics of argumentation, of the production of proof, of the transmission of learning, and of the apprenticeship of the imagination.

It also contributes to elevating all language games to self-knowledge, even those not within the realm of canonical knowledge. It tends to jolt everyday discourse into a kind of metadiscourse: ordinary statements are now displaying a propensity for self-citation, and the various pragmatic posts are tending to make an indirect connection even to current messages concerning them.[217] Finally, it suggests that the problems of internal communication experienced by the scientific community in the course of its work of dismantling and remounting its languages are comparable in nature to the problems experienced by the social collectivity when, deprived of its narrative culture, it must reexamine its own internal communication and in the process question the nature of the legitimacy of the decisions made in its name.

At risk of scandalizing the reader, I would also say that the system can count severity among its advantages. Within the framework of the power criterion, a request (that is, a form of prescription) gains nothing in legitimacy by virtue of being based on the hardship of an unmet need. Rights do not flow from hardship, but from the fact that the alleviation of hardship improves the system's performance. The needs of the most underprivileged should not be used as a system regulator as a matter of principle: since the means of satisfying them is already known, their actual satisfaction will not improve the system's performance, but only increase its expenditures. The only counterindication is that not satisfying them can destabilize the whole. It is against the nature of force to be ruled by weakness. But it is in its nature to induce new requests meant to lead to a redefinition of the norms of "life."[218] In this sense, the system seems to be a vanguard machine dragging humanity after it, dehumanizing it in order to rehumanize it at a different level of normative capacity. The technocrats declare that they cannot trust what society designates as its needs; they "know" that society cannot know its own needs since they are not variables independent of the new technologies.[219] Such is the arrogance of the decision makers—and their blindness.

What their "arrogance" means is that they identify themselves with the social system conceived as a totality in quest of its most performative unity possible. If we look at the pragmatics of science, we learn that such an identification is impossible: in principle, no scientist embodies knowledge or neglects the "needs" of a research project, or the aspirations of a researcher, on the pretext that they do not add to the performance of "science" as a whole. The response a researcher usually makes to a request is: "We'll have to see, tell me your story."[220] In principle, he does not prejudge that a case has already been closed or that the power of "science" will suffer if it is reopened. In fact, the opposite is true.

Of course, it does not always happen like this in reality. Countless scientists have seen their "move" ignored or repressed, sometimes for decades, because it too abruptly destabilized the accepted positions, not only in the university and scientific hierarchy, but also in the problematic.[221] The stronger the "move," the more likely it is to be denied the minimum consensus, precisely because it changes the rules of the game upon which consensus had been based. But when the institution of knowledge functions in this manner, it is acting like an ordinary power center whose behavior is governed by a principle of homeostasis.

Such behavior is terrorist, as is the behavior of the system described by Luhmann. By terror I mean the efficiency gained by eliminating, or threatening to eliminate, a player from the language game one shares with him. He is silenced or consents, not because he has been refuted, but because his ability to participate has been threatened (there are many ways to prevent someone from playing). The decision makers' arrogance, which in principle has no equivalent in the sciences, consists in the exercise of terror. It says: "Adapt your aspirations to our ends—or else."[222]

Even permissiveness toward the various games is made conditional on performativity. The redefinition of the norms of life consists in enhancing the system's competence for power. That this is the case is particularly evident in the introduction of telematics technology: the technocrats see in telematics a promise of liberalization and enrichment in the interactions between interlocutors; but what makes this process attractive for them is that it will result in new tensions in the system, and these will lead to an improvement in its performativity.[223]

To the extent that science is differential, its pragmatics provides the antimodel of a stable system. A statement is deemed worth retaining the moment it marks a difference from what is already known, and after an argument and proof in support of it has been found. Science is a model of an "open system,"[224] in which a statement becomes relevant if it "generates ideas," that is, if it generates other statements and other game rules. Science possesses no general metalanguage in which all other languages can be transcribed and evaluated. This is what prevents its identification with the system and, all things considered, with terror. If the division between decision makers and executors exists in the scientific community (and it does), it is a fact of the socioeconomic system and not of the pragmatics of science itself. It is in fact one of the major obstacles to the imaginative development of knowledge.

The general question of legitimation becomes: What is the relationship between the antimodel of the pragmatics of science and society? Is it applicable to the vast clouds of language material constituting a society? Or is it limited to the game of learning? And if so, what role does it play with respect to the social bond? Is it an impossible ideal of an open community? Is it an essential component for the subset of decision makers, who force on society the performance criterion they reject for themselves. Or, conversely, is it a refusal to cooperate with the authorities, a move in the direction of counterculture, with the attendant risk that all possibility for research will be foreclosed due to lack of funding?[225]

From the beginning of this study, I have emphasized the differences (not only formal, but also pragmatic) between the various language games, especially between denotative, or knowledge, games and prescriptive, or action, games. The pragmatics of science is centered on denotative utterances, which are the foundation upon which it builds institutions of learning (institutes, centers, universities, etc.). But its postmodern development brings a decisive "fact" to the fore: even discussions of denotative statements need to have rules. Rules are not denotative but prescriptive utterances, which we are better off calling metaprescriptive utterances to avoid confusion (they prescribe what the moves of language games must be in order to be admissible). The function of the differential or imaginative or paralogical activity of the current pragmatics of science is to point out these metaprescriptives (science's "presuppositions")[226] and to petition the players to accept different ones. The only legitimation that can make this kind of request admissible is that it will generate ideas, in other words, new statements.

Social pragmatics does not have the "simplicity" of scientific pragmatics. It is a monster formed by the interweaving of various networks of heteromorphous classes of utterances (denotative, prescriptive, performative, technical, evaluative, etc.). There is no reason to think that it would be possible to determine metaprescriptives common to all of these language games or that a revisable consensus like the one in force at a given moment in the scientific community could embrace the totality of metaprescriptions regulating the totality of statements circulating in the social collectivity. As a matter of fact, the contemporary decline of narratives of legitimation—be they traditional or "modern" (the emancipation of humanity, the realization of the Idea)—is tied to the abandonment of this belief. It is its absence for which the ideology of the "system," with its pretensions to totality, tries to compensate and which it expresses in the cynicism of its criterion of performance.

For this reason, it seems neither possible, nor even prudent, to follow Habermas in orienting our treatment of the problem of legitimation in the direction of a search for universal consensus[227] through what he calls *Diskurs*, in other words, a dialogue of argumentation.[228]

This would be to make two assumptions. The first is that it is possible for all speakers to come to agreement on which rules or metaprescriptions are universally valid for language games, when it is clear that language games are heteromorphous, subject to heterogeneous sets of pragmatic rules.

The second assumption is that the goal of dialogue is consensus. But as I have shown in the analysis of the pragmatics of science, consensus is only a particular state of discussion, not its end. Its end, on the contrary, is paralogy. This double observation (the hetero-geneity of the rules and the search for dissent) destroys a belief that still underlies Habermas's research, namely, that humanity as a col-lective (universal) subject seeks its common emancipation through the regularization of the "moves" permitted in all language games and that the legitimacy of any statement resides in its contributing to that emancipation.[229]

It is easy to see what function this recourse plays in Habermas's argument against Luhmann. *Diskurs* is his ultimate weapon against the theory of the stable system. The cause is good, but the argument is not.[230] Consensus has become an outmoded and suspect value. But justice as a value is neither outmoded nor suspect. We must thus arrive at an idea and practice of justice that is not linked to that of consensus.

A recognition of the heteromorphous nature of language games is a first step in that direction. This obviously implies a renunciation of terror, which assumes that they are isomorphic and tries to make them so. The second step is the principle that any consensus on the rules defining a game and the "moves" playable within it *must* be local, in other words, agreed on by its present players and subject to eventual cancellation. The orientation then favors a multiplicity of finite meta-arguments, by which I mean argumentation that con-cerns metaprescriptives and is limited in space and time.

This orientation corresponds to the course that the evolution of social interaction is currently taking; the temporary contract is in practice supplanting permanent institutions in the professional, emotional, sexual, cultural, family, and international domains, as well as in political affairs. This evolution is of course ambiguous: the temporary contract is favored by the system due to its greater flexi-bility, lower cost, and the creative turmoil of its accompanying moti-vations—all of these factors contribute to increased operativity. In any case, there is no question here of proposing a "pure" alternative to the system: we all now know, as the 1970s come to a close, that an attempt at an alternative of that kind would end up resembling the system it was meant to replace. We should be happy that the tendency toward the temporary contract is ambiguous: it is not totally subordinated to the goal of the system, yet the system toler-ates it. This bears witness to the existence of another goal within the system: knowledge of language games as such and the decision to assume responsibility for their rules and effects. Their most signifi-cant effect is precisely what validates the adoption of rules—the quest for paralogy.

We are finally in a position to understand how the computerization of society affects this problematic. It could become the "dream" instrument for controlling and regulating the market system, extended to include knowledge itself and governed exclusively by the performativity principle. In that case, it would inevitably involve the use of terror. But it could also aid groups discussing metaprescriptives by supplying them with the information they usually lack for making knowledgeable decisions. The line to follow for computerization to take the second of these two paths is, in principle, quite simple: give the public free access to the memory and data banks.[231] Language games would then be games of perfect information at any given moment. But they would also be non-zero-sum games, and by virtue of that fact discussion would never risk fixating in a position of minimax equilibrium because it had exhausted its stakes. For the stakes would be knowledge (or information, if you will), and the reserve of knowledge—language's reserve of possible utterances—is inexhaustible. This sketches the outline of a politics that would respect both the desire for justice and the desire for the unknown.

Appendix

Answering the Question:
What Is Postmodernism?
Translated by Régis Durand

A Demand

This is a period of slackening—I refer to the color of the times. From every direction we are being urged to put an end to experimentation, in the arts and elsewhere. I have read an art historian who extols realism and is militant for the advent of a new subjectivity. I have read an art critic who packages and sells "Transavantgardism" in the marketplace of painting. I have read that under the name of postmodernism, architects are getting rid of the Bauhaus project, throwing out the baby of experimentation with the bathwater of functionalism. I have read that a new philosopher is discovering what he drolly calls Judaeo-Christianism, and intends by it to put an end to the impiety which we are supposed to have spread. I have read in a French weekly that some are displeased with *Mille Plateaux* [by Deleuze and Guattari] because they expect, especially when reading a work of philosophy, to be gratified with a little sense. I have read from the pen of a reputable historian that writers and thinkers of the 1960 and 1970 avant-gardes spread a reign of terror in the use of language, and that the conditions for a fruitful exchange must be restored by imposing on the intellectuals a common way of speaking, that of the historians. I have been reading a young philosopher of language who complains that Continental thinking, under the challenge of speaking machines, has surrendered to the machines the concern for reality, that it has substituted for the referential paradigm that of "adlinguisticity" (one speaks about speech, writes about writing, intertextuality), and who thinks that the time has now come to restore a solid anchorage of language in the referent. I have read a talented theatrologist for whom postmodernism, with its games and fantasies, carries very little weight in front of political authority, especially when a worried public opinion encourages authority to a politics of totalitarian surveillance in the face of nuclear warfare threats.

I have read a thinker of repute who defends modernity against those he calls the neoconservatives. Under the banner of postmodernism, the latter would like, he believes, to get rid of the uncompleted project of modernism, that of the Enlightenment. Even the last advocates of *Aufklärung,* such as Popper or Adorno, were only able, according to him, to defend the project in a few particular spheres of life—that of politics for the author of *The Open Society,* and that of art for the author of *Ästhetische Theorie.* Jürgen Habermas (everyone had recognized him) thinks that if modernity has failed, it is in allowing the totality of life to be splintered into independent specialties which are left to the narrow competence of experts, while the concrete individual experiences "desublimated meaning" and "destructured form," not as a liberation but in the mode of that immense *ennui* which Baudelaire described over a century ago.

Following a prescription of Albrecht Wellmer, Habermas considers that the remedy for this splintering of culture and its separation from life can only come from "changing the status of aesthetic experience when it is no longer primarily expressed in judgments of taste," but when it is "used to explore a living historical situation," that is, when "it is put in relation with problems of existence." For this experience then "becomes a part of a language game which is no longer that of aesthetic criticism"; it takes part "in cognitive processes and normative expectations"; "it alters the manner in which those different moments *refer* to one another." What Habermas requires from the arts and the experiences they provide is, in short, to bridge the gap between cognitive, ethical, and political discourses, thus opening the way to a unity of experience.

My question is to determine what sort of unity Habermas has in mind. Is the aim of the project of modernity the constitution of sociocultural unity within which all the elements of daily life and of thought would take their places as in an organic whole? Or does the passage that has to be charted between heterogeneous language games—those of cognition, of ethics, of politics—belong to a different order from that? And if so, would it be capable of effecting a real synthesis between them?

The first hypothesis, of a Hegelian inspiration, does not challenge the notion of a dialectically totalizing *experience;* the second is closer to the spirit of Kant's *Critique of Judgment;* but must be submitted, like the *Critique,* to that severe reexamination which postmodernity imposes on the thought of the Enlightenment, on the idea of a unitary end of history and of a subject. It is this critique which not only Wittgenstein and Adorno have initiated, but also a few other thinkers (French or other) who do not have the honor to be read by Professor Habermas—which at least saves them from getting a poor grade for their neoconservatism.

Realism

The demands I began by citing are not all equivalent. They can even be contradictory. Some are made in the name of postmodernism, others in order to combat it. It is not necessarily the same thing to formulate a demand for some referent (and objective reality), for some sense (and credible transcendence), for an addressee (and audience), or an addressor (and subjective expressiveness) or for some communicational consensus (and a general code of exchanges, such as the genre of historical discourse). But in the diverse invitations to suspend artistic experimentation, there is an identical call for order, a desire for unity, for identity, for security, or popularity (in the sense of *Öffentlichkeit,* of "finding a public"). Artists and writers must be brought back into the bosom of the community, or at least, if the latter is considered to be ill, they must be assigned the task of healing it.

There is an irrefutable sign of this common disposition: it is that for all those writers nothing is more urgent than to liquidate the heritage of the avant-gardes. Such is the case, in particular, of the so-called transavantgardism. The answers given by Achille Bonito Oliva to the questions asked by Bernard Lamarche-Vadel and Michel Enric leave no room for doubt about this. By putting the avant-gardes through a mixing process, the artist and critic feel more confident that they can suppress them than by launching a frontal attack. For they can pass off the most cynical eclecticism as a way of going beyond the fragmentary character of the preceding experiments; whereas if they openly turned their backs on them, they would run the risk of appearing ridiculously neoacademic. The *Salons* and the *Académies,* at the time when the bourgeoisie was establishing itself in history, were able to function as purgation and to grant awards for good plastic and literary conduct under the cover of realism. But capitalism inherently possesses the power to derealize familiar objects, social roles, and institutions to such a degree that the so-called realistic representations can no longer evoke reality except as nostalgia or mockery, as an occasion for suffering rather than for satisfaction. Classicism seems to be ruled out in a world in which reality is so destabilized that it offers no occasion for experience but one for ratings and experimentation.

This theme is familiar to all readers of Walter Benjamin. But it is necessary to assess its exact reach. Photography did not appear as a challenge to painting from the outside, any more than industrial cinema did to narrative literature. The former was only putting the final touch to the program of ordering the visible elaborated by the quattrocento; while the latter was the last step in rounding off diachronies as organic wholes, which had been the ideal of the great novels of education since the eighteenth century. That the mechanical and the industrial should appear as substitutes for hand or craft was not in itself a disaster—except if one believes that art is in its essence the expression of an individuality of genius assisted by an elite craftsmanship.

The challenge lay essentially in that photographic and cinematographic processes can accomplish better, faster, and with a circulation a hundred thousand times larger than narrative or pictorial realism, the task which academicism had assigned to realism: to preserve various consciousnesses from doubt. Industrial photography and cinema will be superior to painting and the novel whenever the objective is to stabilize the referent, to arrange it according to a point of view which endows it with a recognizable meaning, to reproduce the syntax and vocabulary which enable the addressee to decipher images and sequences quickly, and so to arrive easily at the consciousness of his own identity as well as the approval which he thereby receives from others—since such structures of images and sequences constitute a communication code among all of them. This is the way the effects of reality, or if one prefers, the fantasies of realism, multiply.

If they too do not wish to become supporters (of minor importance at that) of what exists, the painter and novelist must refuse to lend themselves to such therapeutic uses. They must question the rules of the art of painting or of narrative as they have learned and received them from their predecessors. Soon those rules must appear to them as a means to deceive, to seduce, and to reassure, which makes it impossible for them to be "true." Under the common name of painting and literature, an unprecedented split is taking place. Those who refuse to reexamine the rules of art pursue successful careers in mass conformism by communicating, by means of the "correct rules," the endemic desire for reality with objects and situations capable of gratifying it. Pornography is the use of photography and film to such an end. It is becoming a general model for the visual or narrative arts which have not met the challenge of the mass media.

As for the artists and writers who question the rules of plastic and narrative arts and possibly share their suspicions by circulating their work, they are destined to have little credibility in the eyes of those concerned with "reality" and "identity"; they have no guarantee of an audience. Thus it is possible to ascribe the dialectics of the avant-gardes to the challenge posed by the realisms of industry and mass communication to painting and the narrative arts. Duchamp's "ready made" does nothing but actively and parodistically signify this constant process of dispossession of the craft of painting or even of being an artist. As Thierry de Duve penetratingly observes, the modern aesthetic question is not "What is beautiful?" but "What can be said to be art (and literature)?"

Realism, whose only definition is that it intends to avoid the question of reality implicated in that of art, always stands somewhere between academicism and kitsch. When power assumes the name of a party, realism and its neoclassical complement triumph over the experimental avant-garde by slandering and banning it—that is, provided the "correct" images, the "correct" narratives, the "correct" forms which the party requests, selects, and propagates can find a public to desire them as the appropriate remedy for the anxiety and depression that public experiences. The demand for reality—that is, for unity, simplicity, communicability, etc.—did not have the same intensity nor the same continuity in German society between the two world wars and in Russian society after the Revolution: this provides a basis for a distinction between Nazi and Stalinist realism.

What is clear, however, is that when it is launched by the political apparatus, the attack on artistic experimentation is specifically reactionary: aesthetic judgment would only be required to decide whether such or such work is in conformity with the established rules of the beautiful. Instead of the work of art having to investigate what makes it an art object and whether it will be able to find an audience, political academicism possesses and imposes a priori criteria of the beautiful, which designate some works and a public at a stroke and forever. The use of categories in aesthetic judgment would thus be of the same nature as in cognitive judgment. To speak like Kant, both would be determining judgments: the expression is "well formed" first in the understanding, then the only cases retained in experience are those which can be subsumed under this expression.

When power is that of capital and not that of a party, the "trans-avantgardist" or "postmodern" (in Jencks's sense) solution proves to be better adapted than the antimodern solution. Eclecticism is the degree zero of contemporary general culture: one listens to reggae, watches a western, eats McDonald's food for lunch and local cuisine for dinner, wears Paris perfume in Tokyo and "retro" clothes in Hong Kong; knowledge is a matter for TV games. It is easy to find a public for eclectic works. By becoming kitsch, art panders to the confusion which reigns in the "taste" of the patrons. Artists, gallery owners, critics, and public wallow together in the "anything goes," and the epoch is one of slackening. But this realism of the "anything goes" is in fact that of money; in the absence of aesthetic criteria, it remains possible and useful to assess the value of works of art according to the profits they yield. Such realism accommodates all tendencies, just as capital accommodates all "needs," providing that the tendencies and needs have purchasing power. As for taste, there is no need to be delicate when one speculates or entertains oneself.

Artistic and literary research is doubly threatened, once by the "cultural policy" and once by the art and book market. What is advised, sometimes through one channel, sometimes through the other, is to offer works which, first, are relative to subjects which exist in the eyes of the public they address, and second, works so made ("well made") that the public will recognize what they are about, will understand what is signified, will be able to give or refuse its approval knowingly, and if possible, even to derive from such work a certain amount of comfort.

The interpretation which has just been given of the contact between the industrial and mechanical arts, and literature and the fine arts is correct in its outline, but it remains narrowly sociologizing and his-toricizing—in other words, one-sided. Stepping over Benjamin's and Adorno's reticences, it must be recalled that science and industry are no more free of the suspicion which concerns reality than are art and writing. To believe otherwise would be to entertain an excessively humanistic notion of the mephistophelian functionalism of sciences and technologies. There is no denying the dominant existence today of techno-science, that is, the massive subordination of cognitive statements to the finality of the best possible performance, which is the technological criterion. But the mechanical and the industrial, especially when they enter fields traditionally reserved for artists, are carrying with them much more than power effects. The objects and the thoughts which originate in scientific knowledge and the capitalist economy convey with them one of the rules which supports their possibility: the rule that there is no reality unless testified by a consensus between partners over a certain knowledge and certain commitments.

This rule is of no little consequence. It is the imprint left on the politics of the scientist and the trustee of capital by a kind of flight of reality out of the metaphysical, religious, and political certainties that the mind believed it held. This withdrawal is absolutely necessary to the emergence of science and capitalism. No industry is possible without a suspicion of the Aristotelian theory of motion, no industry without a refutation of corporatism, of mercantilism, and of physiocracy. Modernity, in whatever age it appears, cannot exist without a shattering of belief and without discovery of the "lack of reality" of reality, together with the invention of other realities.

What does this "lack of reality" signify if one tries to free it from a narrowly historicized interpretation? The phrase is of course akin to what Nietzsche calls nihilism. But I see a much earlier modulation of Nietzschean perspectivism in the Kantian theme of the sublime. I think in particular that it is in the aesthetic of the sublime that modern art (including literature) finds its impetus and the logic of avant-gardes finds its axioms.

The sublime sentiment, which is also the sentiment of the sublime, is, according to Kant, a strong and equivocal emotion: it carries with it both pleasure and pain. Better still, in it pleasure derives from pain. Within the tradition of the subject, which comes from Augustine and Descartes and which Kant does not radically challenge, this contradiction, which some would call neurosis or masochism, develops as a conflict between the faculties of a subject, the faculty to conceive of something and the faculty to "present" something. Knowledge exists if, first, the statement is intelligible, and second, if "cases" can be derived from the experience which "corresponds" to it. Beauty exists if a certain "case" (the work of art), given first by the sensibility without any conceptual determination, the sentiment of pleasure independent of any interest the work may elicit, appeals to the principle of a universal consensus (which may never be attained).

Taste, therefore, testifies that between the capacity to conceive and the capacity to present an object corresponding to the concept, an undetermined agreement, without rules, giving rise to a judgment which Kant calls reflective, may be experienced as pleasure. The sublime is a different sentiment. It takes place, on the contrary, when the imagination fails to present an object which might, if only in principle, come to match a concept. We have the Idea of the world (the totality of what is), but we do not have the capacity to show an example of it. We have the Idea of the simple (that which cannot be broken down, decomposed), but we cannot illustrate it with a sensible object which would be a "case" of it. We can conceive the infinitely great, the infinitely powerful, but every presentation of an object destined to "make visible" this absolute greatness or power appears to us painfully inadequate. Those are Ideas of which no presentation is possible. Therefore, they impart no knowledge about reality (experience); they also prevent the free union of the faculties which gives rise to the sentiment of the beautiful; and they prevent the formation and the stabilization of taste. They can be said to be unpresentable.

I shall call modern the art which devotes its "little technical expertise" (son "petit technique"), as Diderot used to say, to present the fact that the unpresentable exists. To make visible that there is something which can be conceived and which can neither be seen nor made visible: this is what is at stake in modern painting. But how to make visible that there is something which cannot be seen? Kant himself shows the way when he names "formlessness, the absence of form," as a possible index to the unpresentable. He also says of the empty "abstraction" which the imagination experiences when in search for a presentation of the infinite (another unpresentable): this abstraction itself is like a presentation of the infinite, its "negative presentation." He cites the commandment, "Thou shalt not make graven images" (Exodus), as the most sublime passage in the Bible in that it forbids all presentation of the Absolute. Little needs to be added to those observations to outline an aesthetic of sublime paintings. As painting, it will of course "present" something though negatively; it will therefore avoid figuration or representation. It will be "white" like one of Malevitch's squares; it will enable us to see only by making it impossible to see; it will please only by causing pain. One recognizes in those instructions the axioms of avant-gardes in painting, inasmuch as they devote themselves to making an allusion to the unpresentable by means of visible presentations. The systems in the name of which, or with which, this task has been able to support or to justify itself deserve the greatest attention; but they can originate only in the vocation of the sublime in order to legitimize it, that is, to conceal it. They remain inexplicable without the incommensurability of reality to concept which is implied in the Kantian philosophy of the sublime.

It is not my intention to analyze here in detail the manner in which the various avant-gardes have, so to speak, humbled and disqualified reality by examining the pictorial techniques which are so many devices to make us believe in it. Local tone, drawing, the mixing of colors, linear perspective, the nature of the support and that of the instrument, the treatment, the display, the museum: the avant-gardes are perpetually flushing out artifices of presentation which make it possible to subordinate thought to the gaze and to turn it away from the unpresentable. If Habermas, like Marcuse, understands this task of derealization as an aspect of the (repressive) "desublimation" which characterizes the avant-garde, it is because he confuses the Kantian sublime with Freudian sublimation, and because aesthetics has remained for him that of the beautiful.

The Postmodern

What, then, is the postmodern? What place does it or does it not occupy in the vertiginous work of the questions hurled at the rules of image and narration? It is undoubtedly a part of the modern. All that has been received, if only yesterday (*modo, modo,* Petronius used to say), must be suspected. What space does Cézanne challenge? The Impressionists'. What object do Picasso and Braque attack? Cézanne's. What presupposition does Duchamp break with in 1912? That which says one must make a painting, be it cubist. And Buren questions that other presupposition which he believes had survived untouched by the work of Duchamp: the place of presentation of the work. In an amazing acceleration, the generations precipitate themselves. A work can become modern only if it is first postmodern. Postmodernism thus understood is not modernism at its end but in the nascent state, and this state is constant.

Yet I would like not to remain with this slightly mechanistic meaning of the word. If it is true that modernity takes place in the withdrawal of the real and according to the sublime relation between the presentable and the conceivable, it is possible, within this relation, to distinguish two modes (to use the musician's language). The emphasis can be placed on the powerlessness of the faculty of presentation, on the nostalgia for presence felt by the human subject, on the obscure and futile will which inhabits him in spite of everything. The emphasis can be placed, rather, on the power of the faculty to conceive, on its "inhumanity" so to speak (it was the quality Apollinaire demanded of modern artists), since it is not the business of our understanding whether or not human sensibility or imagination can match what it conceives. The emphasis can also be placed on the increase of being and the jubilation which result from the invention of new rules of the game, be it pictorial, artistic, or any other. What I have in mind will become clear if we dispose very schematically a few names on the chessboard of the history of avant-gardes: on the side of melancholia, the German Expressionists, and on the side of *novatio*, Braque and Picasso, on the former Malevitch and on the latter Lissitsky, on the one Chirico and on the other Duchamp. The nuance which distinguishes these two modes may be infinitesimal; they often coexist in the same piece, are almost indistinguishable; and yet they testify to a difference (*un différend*) on which the fate of thought depends and will depend for a long time, between regret and assay.

The work of Proust and that of Joyce both allude to something which does not allow itself to be made present. Allusion, to which Paolo Fabbri recently called my attention, is perhaps a form of expression indispensable to the works which belong to an aesthetic of the sublime. In Proust, what is being eluded as the price to pay for this allusion is the identity of consciousness, a victim to the excess of time (*au trop de temps*). But in Joyce, it is the identity of writing which is the victim of an excess of the book (*au trop de livre*) or of literature.

Proust calls forth the unpresentable by means of a language unaltered in its syntax and vocabulary and of a writing which in many of its operators still belongs to the genre of novelistic narration. The literary institution, as Proust inherits it from Balzac and Flaubert, is admittedly subverted in that the hero is no longer a character but the inner consciousness of time, and in that the diegetic diachrony, already damaged by Flaubert, is here put in question because of the narrative voice. Nevertheless, the unity of the book, the odyssey of that consciousness, even if it is deferred from chapter to chapter, is not seriously challenged: the identity of the writing with itself throughout the labyrinth of the interminable narration is enough to connote such unity, which has been compared to that of *The Phenomenology of Mind*.

Joyce allows the unpresentable to become perceptible in his writing itself, in the signifier. The whole range of available narrative and even stylistic operators is put into play without concern for the unity of the whole, and new operators are tried. The grammar and vocabulary of literary language are no longer accepted as given;

rather, they appear as academic forms, as rituals originating in piety (as Nietzsche said) which prevent the unpresentable from being put forward.

Here, then, lies the difference: modern aesthetics is an aesthetic of the sublime, though a nostalgic one. It allows the unpresentable to be put forward only as the missing contents; but the form, because of its recognizable consistency, continues to offer to the reader or viewer matter for solace and pleasure. Yet these sentiments do not constitute the real sublime sentiment, which is in an intrinsic combination of pleasure and pain: the pleasure that reason should exceed all presentation, the pain that imagination or sensibility should not be equal to the concept.

The postmodern would be that which, in the modern, puts forward the unpresentable in presentation itself; that which denies itself the solace of good forms, the consensus of a taste which would make it possible to share collectively the nostalgia for the unattainable; that which searches for new presentations, not in order to enjoy them but in order to impart a stronger sense of the unpresentable. A postmodern artist or writer is in the position of a philosopher: the text he writes, the work he produces are not in principle governed by preestablished rules, and they cannot be judged according to a determining judgment, by applying familiar categories to the text or to the work. Those rules and categories are what the work of art itself is looking for. The artist and the writer, then, are working without rules in order to formulate the rules of what *will have been done.* Hence the fact that work and text have the characters of an *event;* hence also, they always come too late for their author, or, what amounts to the same thing, their being put into work, their realization (*mise en oeuvre*) always begin too soon. *Post modern* would have to be understood according to the paradox of the future (*post*) anterior (*modo*).

It seems to me that the essay (Montaigne) is postmodern, while the fragment (*The Athaeneum*) is modern.

Finally, it must be clear that it is our business not to supply reality but to invent allusions to the conceivable which cannot be presented. And it is not to be expected that this task will effect the last reconciliation between language games (which, under the name of faculties, Kant knew to be separated by a chasm), and that only the transcendental illusion (that of Hegel) can hope to totalize them into a real unity. But Kant also knew that the price to pay for such an illusion is terror. The nineteenth and twentieth centuries have given us as much terror as we can take. We have paid a high enough price for the nostalgia of the whole and the one, for the reconciliation of the concept and the sensible, of the transparent and the communicable experience. Under the general demand for slackening and for appeasement, we can hear the mutterings of the desire for a return of terror, for the realization of the fantasy to seize reality. The answer is: Let us wage a war on totality; let us be witnesses to the unpresentable; let us activate the differences and save the honor of the name.

Notes

Notes

1. Alain Touraine, *La Société postindustrielle* (Paris: Denoël, 1969) [Eng. trans. Leonard Mayhew, *The Post-Industrial Society* (London: Wildwood House, 1974)] ; Daniel Bell, *The Coming of Post-Industrial Society* (New York: Basic Books, 1973); Ihab Hassan, *The Dismemberment of Orpheus: Toward a Post Modern Literature* (New York: Oxford University Press, 1971); Michel Benamou and Charles Caramello, eds., *Performance in Postmodern Culture* (Wisconsin: Center for Twentieth Century Studies & Coda Press, 1977); M. Köhler, "Postmodernismus: ein begriffgeschichtlicher Überblick," *Amerikastudien* 22, 1 (1977).

2. An already classic literary expression of this is provided in Michel Butor, *Mobile: Etude pour une représentation des Etats-Unis* (Paris: Gallimard, 1962).

3. Jib Fowles, ed., *Handbook of Futures Research* (Westport, Conn.: Greenwood Press, 1978).

4. Nikolai S. Trubetskoi, *Grundzüge der Phonologie* (Prague: Travaux du cercle linguistique de Prague, vol. 7, 1939) [Eng. trans. Christiane Baltaxe, *Principles of Phonology* (Berkeley: University of California Press, 1969)] .

5. Norbert Wiener, *Cyberbetics and Society: The Human Use of Human Beings* (Boston: Houghton Mifflin, 1949); William Ross Ashby, *An Introduction to Cyberbetics* (London: Chapman & Hall, 1956).

6. See the work of Johannes von Neumann (1903-57).

7. S. Bellert, "La Formalisation des systèmes cybernétiques," in *Le Concept d'information dans la science contemporaine* (Paris: Minuit, 1965).

8. Georges Mounin, *Les Problèmes théoriques de la traduction* (Paris: Gallimard, 1963). The computer revolution dates from 1965, with the new generation of IBM 360s: R. Moch, "Le Tournant informatique," *Documents contributifs*, Annex 4, *L'Informatisation de la société* (Paris: La Documentation française, 1978); R.M. Ashby, "La Seconde Génération de la micro-électronique," *La Recherche* 2 (June 1970): 127ff.

9. C. L. Gaudfernan and A. Taïb, "Glossaire," in P. Nora and A. Minc, *L'Informatisation de la société* (Paris: La Documentation française, 1978); R. Béca, "Les Banques de données,"

85

Nouvelle informatique et nouvelle croissance, Annex 1, *L'Informatisation de la société*.

10. L. Joyeux, "Les Applications avancées de l'informatique," *Documents contributifs*. Home terminals (Integrated Video Terminals) will be commercialized before 1984 and will cost about $1,400, according to a report of the International Resource Development: *The Home Terminal* (Conn.: I.R.D. Press, 1979).

11. Paul Watzlawick, Janet Helmick-Beavin, Don D. Jackson, *Pragmatics of Human Communication: A Study of Interactional Patterns, Pathologies, and Paradoxes* (New York: Norton, 1967).

12. J. M. Treille, of the Groupe d'analyse et de prospective des systèmes économiques et technologiques (GAPSET), states that, "Not enough has been said about the new possibilities for disseminating stored information, in particular, using semiconductor and laser technology. . . . Soon everyone will be able to store information cheaply wherever he wishes, and, further, will be able to process it autonomously" (*La Semaine media* 16, 16 February 1979). According to a study by the National Science Foundation, more than one high school student in two has ready access to the services of a computer, and all schools will have one in the early 1980s (*La Semaine media* 13, 25 January 1979).

13. L. Brunel, *Des Machines et des hommes* (Montréal: Québec Science, 1978): Jean-Louis Missika and Dominique Wolton, *Les réseaux pensants* (Librairie technique et documentaire, 1978). The use of videoconferences between the province of Quebec and France is becoming routine: in November and December 1978 the fourth series of videoconferences (relayed by the satellite "Symphonie") took place between Quebec and Montreal on the one hand, and Paris (Université Paris Nord and the Beaubourg Center) on the other (*La Semaine media* 5, 30 November 1978). Another example is provided by electronic journalism. The three big American networks (ABC, NBC, and CBS) have increased the number of production studios around the world to the extent that almost all the events that occur can now be processed electronically and transmitted to the United States by satellite. Only the Moscow offices still work on film, which is sent to Frankfurt for satellite transmission. London has become the great "packing point" (*La Semaine media* 20, 15 March 1979). [TRANS: For Lyotard's usage of the words *learning* and *knowledge*, see sec. 6 of this text and note 65.]

14. The unit of information is the bit. For these definitions see Gaudfernan and Taïb, "Glossaire." This is discussed in René Thom, "Un protée de la sémantique: l'information" (1973), in *Modèles mathématiques de la morphogenèse* (Paris: Union Générale d'Edition, 1974). In particular, the transcription of messages into code allows ambiguities to be eliminated: see Watzlawick et al., *Pragmatics of Human Communication*, p. 98.

15. The firms Craig and Lexicon have announced the commercial production of pocket translators: four modules for four different languages with simultaneous reception, each containing 1,500 words, with memory. Weidner Communication Systems Inc. produces a *Multilingual Word Processor* that allows the capacity of an average translator to be increased from 600 to 2,400 words per hour. It includes a triple memory: bilingual dictionary, dictionary of synonyms, grammatical index (*La Semaine media* 6, 6 December 1978, 5).

16. Jürgen Habermas, *Erkenntnis und Interesse* (Frankfurt: Suhrkamp, 1968) [Eng. trans. Jeremy Shapiro, *Knowledge and Human Interests* (Boston: Beacon, 1971)].

17. "Man's understanding of nature and his mastery over it by virtue of his presence as a social body . . . appears as the great foundation-stone [*Grundpfeiler*] of production and of wealth," so that "general social knowledge becomes a *direct force of production*," writes Marx in the *Grundrisse* (1857-58) [(Berlin: Dietz Verlag, 1953), p. 593; Eng. trans. Martin Nicolaus (New York: Vintage, 1973), p. 705]. However, Marx concedes that it is not "only in the form of knowledge, but also as immediate organs of social practice" that learning becomes force, in other words, as machines: machines are *"organs of the human brain created by the human hand; the power of knowledge, objectified"* [p. 706]. See Paul Mattick, *Marx and Keynes: The Limits of the Mixed Economy* (Boston: Extending Horizons Books,

1969). This point is discussed in Lyotard, "La place de l'aliénation dans le retournement marxiste" (1969), in *Dérive à partir de Marx et Freud* (Paris: Union Générale d'Edition 1973), pp. 78-166.

18. The composition of the labor force in the United States changed as follows over a twenty-year period (1950-71):

	1950	1971
Factory, service sector, or agricultural workers	62.5%	51.4%
Professionals and technicians	7.5	14.2
White-collar	30.0	34.0

(*Statistical Abstracts,* 1971)

19. Because of the time required for the "fabrication" of a high-level technician or the average scientist in comparison to the time needed to extract raw materials and transfer money-capital. At the end of the 1960s, Mattick estimated the net rate of investment in underdeveloped countries at 3-5% of the GNP and at 10-15% in the developed countries [*Marx and Keynes,* p. 248.]

20. Nora and Minc, *L'Informatisation de la société,* especially pt. 1, "Les défis;" Y. Stourdzé, "Les Etats-Unis et la guerre des communications," *Le Monde,* 13-15 December 1978. In 1979, the value of the world market of telecommunications devices was $30 billion; it is estimated that in ten years it will reach $68 billion (*La Semaine media* 19, 8 March 1979).

21. F. De Combret, "Le redéploiement industriel," *Le Monde,* April 1978; M. Lepage, *Demain le capitalisme* (Paris: Le Livre de Poche, 1978); Alain Cotta, *La France et l'impératif mondial* (Paris: Presses Universitaires de France, 1978).

22. It is a matter of "weakening the administration," of reaching the "minimal state." This is the decline of the Welfare State, which is accompanying the "crisis" that began in 1974.

23. "La Nouvelle informatique et ses utilisateurs," Annex 3, *L'Informatisation de la société* (note 8).

24. B. P. Lécuyer, "Bilan et perspectives de la sociologie des sciences dans les pays occidentaux," *Archives européennes de sociologie* 19 (1978):257-336 (bibliography). Good information on English and American currents: the hegemony of Merton's school until the beginning of the 1970s and the current dispersion, especially under the influence of Kuhn; not much information on German sociology of science.

25. The term has been given weight by Ivan Illich, *Tools for Conviviality* (New York, Harper & Row, 1973).

26. On this "demoralization", see A. Jaubert and J.-M. Lévy-Leblond, eds., *(Auto) critique de la science* (Paris: Seuil, 1973), Pt. 1.

27. Jürgen Habermas, *Legitimationsprobleme im Spätkapitalismus* (Frankfurt: Suhrkamp, 1973) [Eng. trans. Thomas McCarthy, *Letimation Crisis* (Boston: Beacon Press, 1975)].

28. In the wake of Peirce's semiotics, the distinction of the syntactic, semantic, and pragmatic domains is made by Charles W. Morris, "Foundations of the Theory of Signs," in Otto Neurath, Rudolph Carnap, and Charles Morris, eds., *International Encyclopedia of Unified Science,* vol. 1, pt. 2 (1938): 77-137. For the use of this term I refer especially to: Ludwig Wittgenstein, *Philosophical Investigations* [trans. G. E. M. Anscombe (New York: Macmillan, 1953)]; J. L. Austin, *How to Do Things with Words* (Oxford: Oxford University Press, 1962); J. R. Searle, *Speech Acts* (Cambridge: Cambridge University Press, 1969); Jürgen Habermas, "Unbereitende Bermerkungen zu einer Theorie der kommunikativen Kompetens," in Habermas and Luhmann, *Theorie der gesellschaft oder Sozialtechnologie* (Stuttgart: Suhrkamp, 1971); Oswald Ducrot, *Dire et ne pas dire* (Paris: Hermann, 1972); J. Poulain, "Vers une pragmatique nucléaire de la communication" (typescript, Université de Montréal, 1977). See too Watzlawick et al. *Pragmatics of Human Communication* (note 11).

29. "Denotation" corresponds here to "description" in the classical usage of logicians. Quine replaces "denotation" by "true of"; see W. V. Quine, *Word and Object* (Cambridge, Mass.: MIT Press, 1960). J. L. Austin, *How to Do Things with Words*, p. 39, prefers "constative" to "descriptive."

30. The term *performative* has taken on a precise meaning in language theory since Austin, Later in this book, the concept will reappear in association with the term *performativity* (in particular, of a system) in the new current sense of efficiency measured according to an input/output ratio. The two meanings are not far apart. Austin's performative realizes the optimal performance.

31. A recent analysis of these categories is to be found in Habermas, "Unbereitende Bemerkungen," and is discussed by J. Poulain, "Vers une pragmatique nucléaire."

32. *Philosophical Investigations*, sec. 23.

33. John Von Neumann and Oskar Morgenstern, *Theory of Games and Economic Behavior* (Princeton University Press, 1944), p. 49: "The *game* is simply the totality of the rules which describe it." This formulation is foreign to the spirit of Wittgenstein, for whom the concept of the game cannot be mastered by a definition, since definition is already a language game (*Philosophical Investigations*, especially secs. 65-84).

34. The term comes from Searle: "Speech acts . . . are the basic or minimal units of linguistic communication" [*Speech Acts*, p. 16]. I place them within the domain of the *agon* (the joust) rather than that of communication.

35. Agonistics is the basis of Heraclitus's ontology and of the Sophists' dialectic, not to mention the early tragedians. A good part of Aristotle's reflections in the *Topics* and the *Sophistici Elenchi* is devoted to it. See F. Nietzsche, "Homer's Contest" [trans. Maximilian A. Mügge, in *Complete Works*, vol. 2 (London: T. N. Fowlis, 1911; reprint, New York: Gordon Press, 1974)].

36. In the sense established by Louis Hjelmslev, in *Prolegomena to a Theory of Language* (Madison: University of Wisconsin Press, 1963), and taken up by Roland Barthes, *Eléments de sémiologie* (1964) (Paris: Seuil, 1966), 4:1 [Eng. trans. Annette Lavers and Colin Smith, *Elements of Semiology* (New York: Hill and Wang, 1968)].

37. See in particular Tallcott Parsons, *The Social System* (Glencoe, Ill.: Free Press, 1967), and *Sociological Theory and Modern Society* (New York: Free Press, 1967). A bibliography of Marxist theory of contemporary society would fill more than fifty pages. The reader can consult the useful summary (dossiers and critical bibliography) provided by Pierre Souyri, *Le Marxisme après Marx* (Paris: Flammarion, 1970). An interesting view of the conflict between these two great currents of social theory and of their intermixing is given by A. W. Gouldner, *The Coming Crisis of Western Sociology* (New York: Basic Books, 1970). This conflict occupies an important place in the thought of Habermas, who is simultaneously the heir of the Frankfurt School and in a polemical relationship with the German theory of the social system, especially that of Luhmann.

38. This optimism appears clearly in the conclusions of Robert Lynd, *Knowledge for What?* (Princeton, N.J.: Princeton University Press, 1939), p. 239; quoted by Max Horkheimer, *Eclipse of Reason* (Oxford: Oxford University Press, 1947): in modern society, science must replace religion ("worn threadbare") in defining the aims of life.

39. Helmut Schelsky, *Der Mensch in der Wissenschaftlichen Zivilisation* (Köln und Opladen: Arbeitsgemeinschaft für Forschung des Landes Nordrhein-Westfalen, Geisteswissenschaften Heft 96), pp. 24ff: "The sovereignty of the State is no longer manifested by simple fact that it monopolizes the use of violence (Max Weber) or possesses emergency powers (Carl Schmitt), but primarily by the fact that the State determines the degree of effectiveness of all of the technical means existing within it, reserving their greatest effectiveness for itself, while at the same time exempting its own use of these instruments from the limitations it applies to their use by others." It will be said that this is a theory of the

State, not of the system. But Schelsky adds: "In the process, the State's choice of goals is subordinated to the law that I have already mentioned as being the universal law of scientific civilization: namely that the means determine the ends, or rather, that the technical possibilities dictate what use is made of them." Habermas invokes against this law the fact that sets of technical means and systems of finalized rational action never develop autonomously: cf. "Dogmatism, Reason, and Decision: On Theory and Practice in Our Scientific Civilization" [trans. John Viertel, in *Theory and Practice* (Boston: Beacon, 1973)]. See too Jacques Ellul, *La Technique ou l'enjeu du siècle* (Paris: Armand Colin, 1954), and *Le Système technicien* (Paris: Calmann-Lévy, 1977). That strikes, and in general the strong pressure brought to bear by powerful workers' organizations, produce a tension that is in the long run beneficial to the performance of the system is stated clearly by C. Levinson, a union leader; he attributes the technical and managerial advance of American industry to this tension (quoted by H.-F. de Virieu, *Le Matin*, special number, "Que veut Giscard?" December 1978).

40. Talcott Parsons, *Essays in Sociological Theory Pure and Applied*, rev. ed. (Glencoe, Ill.: Free Press, 1954), pp. 216-18.

41. I am using this word in the sense of John Kenneth Galbraith's term *technostructure* as presented in *The New Industrial State* (Boston: Houghton Mifflin, 1967), or Raymond Aron's term *technico-bureaucratic structure* in *Dix-huit leçons sur la société industrielle* (Paris: Gallimard, 1962) [Eng. trans. M. K. Bottomore, *Eighteen Lectures on Industrial Society* (London: Weidenfeld and Nicholson, 1967)], not in a sense associated with the term *bureaucracy*. The term *bureaucracy* is much "harder" because it is sociopolitical as much as it is economical, and because it descends from the critique of Bolshevik power by the worker's Opposition (Kollontaï) and the critique of Stalinism by the Trotskyist opposition. See on this subject Claude Lefort, *Eléments d'une critique de la bureaucratie* (Genève: Droz, 1971), in which the critique is extended to bureaucratic society as a whole.

42. *Eclipse of Reason*, p. 183.

43. Max Horkheimer, "Traditionnelle und kritische Theorie" (1937), [Eng. trans. in J. O'Connell et al., trans., *Critical Theory. Selected Essays* (New York: Herder & Herder, 1972)].

44. See Claude Lefort, *Eléments d'une critique*, and *Un homme en trop* (Paris: Seuil, 1976 1976); Cornelius Castoriadis, *La Société bureaucratique* (Paris: Union Générale d'Edition, 1973).

45. See for example J. P. Garnier, *Le Marxisme lénifiant* (Paris: Le Sycomore, 1979).

46. This was the title of the "organ of critique and revolutionary orientation" published between 1949 and 1965 by a group whose principal editors, under various pseudonyms, were C. de Beaumont, D. Blanchard, C. Castoriadis, S. de Diesbach, C. Le'ort, J.-F. Lyotard, A. Maso, D. Mothé, P. Simon, P. Souyri.

47. Ernest Bloch, *Das Prinzip Hoffnung* (Frankfurt: Suhrkamp Verlag, 1959). See G. Raulet, ed., *Utopie-Marxisme selon E. Bloch* (Paris: Payot, 1976).

48. This is an allusion to the theoretical bunglings occasioned by the Algerian and Vietnam wars, and the student movement of the 1960s. A historical survey of these is given by Alain Schapp and Pierre Vidal-Naquet in their introduction to the *Journal de la Commune étudiante* (Paris: Seuil, 1969) [Eng. trans. Maria Jolas, *The French Student Uprising, November 1967-June 1968* (Boston: Beacon, 1971)].

49. Lewis Mumford, *The Myth of the Machine: Technics and Human Development*, 2 vols. (New York: Harcourt, Brace, 1967).

50. An appeal that was intended to secure intellectuals' participation in the system is nonetheless imbued with hesitation between these two hypotheses: P. Nemo, "La Nouvelle Responsabilité des clercs," *Le Monde*, 8 September 1978.

51. The origin of the theoretical opposition between *Naturwissenschaft* and *Geisteswissenschaft* is to be found in the work of Wilhelm Dilthey (1863-1911).

52. M. Albert, a commission member of the French Plan, writes: "The Plan is a governmental research department. . . . It is also a great meeting place where ideas ferment, where points of view clash and where change is prepared. . . . We must not be alone. Others must enlighten us. . . . " (*L'Expansion*, November 1978). On the problem of decision, see G. Gafgen, *Theorie der wissenschaftlichen Entscheidung* (Tübingen, 1963); L. Sfez *Critique de la décision* (1973; Presses de la Fondation nationale des sciences politiques, 1976).

53. Think of the waning of names such as Stalin, Mao, and Castro as the eponyms of revolution over the last twenty years; consider the erosion of the image of the president in the United States since the Watergate affair.

54. This is a central theme in Robert Musil, *Der Mann ohne Eigenschaften* (1930-33; Hamburg: Rowolt, 1952) [Eng. trans. Eithne Wilkins and Ernest Kaiser, *The Man without Qualities* (London: Secker and Warburg, 1953-60)]. In a free commentary, J. Bouveresse underlines the affinity of this theme of the "dereliction" of the self with the "crisis" of science at the beginning of the twentieth century and with Mach's epistemology; he cites the following evidence: "Given the state of science in particular, a man is made only of what people say he is or of what is done with what he is. . . . The world is one in which lived events have become independent of man. . . . It is a world of happening, of what happens without its happening to anyone, and without anyone's being responsible" ("La problématique du sujet dans *L'Homme sans qualités*," *Noroît* (Arras) 234 and 235 (December 1978 and January 1979); the published text was not revised by the author.

55. Jean Baudrillard, *A l'ombre des majorités silencieuses, ou la fin du social* (Fontenay-sous-bois: Cahiers Utopie 4, 1978) [Eng. trans. *In the Shadow of the Silent Majority* (New York: Semiotexte, 1983)].

56. This is the vocabulary of systems theory. See for example P. Nemo, "La Nouvelle Responsabilité": "Think of society as a system, in the cybernetic sense. This system is a communication grid with intersections where messages converge and are redistributed. . . ."

57. An example of this is given by J.-P. Garnier, *Le Marxisme lénifiant*, "The role of the Center for Information on Social Innovation, directed by H. Dougier and F. Bloch-Lainé, is to inventory, analyze, and distribute information on new experiences of daily life (education, health, justice, cultural activities, town planning and architecture, etc.). This data bank on 'alternative practices' lends its services to those state organs whose job it is to see to it that 'civil society' remains a civilized society: the Commissariat au Plan, the Secrétariat à l'action sociale, DATAR, etc."

58. Freud in particular stressed this form of "predestination." See Marthe Robert, *Roman des origines, origine du roman* (Paris: Grasset, 1972).

59. See the work of Michel Serres, especially *Hermès I-IV* (Paris: Editions de Minuit, 1969-77).

60. For example, Erving Goffman, *The Presentation of Self in Everyday Life* (Garden City, N.Y.: Doubleday, 1959); Gouldner, *The Coming Crisis* (note 37), chap. 10; Alain Touraine et al., *Lutte étudiante* (Paris: Seuil, 1978); M. Callon, "Sociologie des techniques?" *Pandore* 2 (February 1979): 28-32; Watzlawick et al., *Pragmatics of Human Communication* (note 11).

61. See note 41. The theme of general bureaucratization as the future of modern societies was first developed by B. Rizzi, *La Bureaucratisation du monde* (Paris: B. Rizzi, 1939).

62. See H. P. Grice, "Logic and Conversation" in Peter Cole and Jeremy Morgan, eds., *Speech Acts III, Syntax and Semantics* (New York: Academic Press, 1975), pp. 59-82.

63. For a phenomenological approach to the problem, see Maurice Merleau-Ponty, *Résumés de cours*, ed. Claude Lefort (Paris: Gallimard, 1968), the course for 1954-55. For a psychosociological approach, see R. Loureau, *L'Analyse institutionnnelle* (Paris: Editions de Minuit, 1970).

64. M. Callon, "Sociologie des techniques?" p. 30: "Sociologics is the movement by

which actors constitute and institute differences, or frontiers, between what is social and what is not, what is technical and what is not, what is imaginary and what is real: the outline of these frontiers is open to dispute, and no consensus can be achieved except in cases of total domination." Compare this with what Alain Touraine calls permanent sociology in *La Voix et le regard.*

65. The object of knowledge in Aristotle is strictly circumscribed by what he defines as apophantics: "While every sentence has meaning *(semantikos)* . . . not all can be called propositions *(apophantikos).* We call propositions those only that have truth or falsity in them. A prayer is, for instance, a sentence, but neither has truth nor has falsity." "De Interpretatione," 4, 17a, *The Organon,* vol. 1, trans. Harold Cooke and Hugh Tredennick (Cambridge, Mass.: Harvard, 1938), 121. [TRANS: The translation of *connaissance* as "learning" is not uniform. It was sometimes necessary to translate it as "knowledge" (especially where it occurs in the plural); it should be clear from the context whether it is a question of *connaissance* (in Lyotard's usage, a body of established denotive statements) or *savoir* (knowledge in the more general sense). *Savoir* has been uniformly translated as "knowledge."]

66. See Karl Popper, *Logik der Forschung* (Wien: Springer, 1935) [Eng. trans. Popper et al., *The Logic of Scientific Discovery* (New York: Basic Books, 1949)], and "Normal Science and its Dangers," in Imre Lakatos and Alan Musgrave, eds., *Criticism and the Growth of Knowledge* (Cambridge: Cambridge University Press, 1970).

67. See Jean Beaufret, *Le Poème de Parménide* (Paris: Presses Universitaires de France, 1955).

68. Again in the sense of *Bildung* (or, in English, "culture"), as accredited by culturalism. The term is preromantic and romantic; cf. Hegel's *Volksgeist.*

69. See the American culturalist school: Cora DuBois, Abram Kardiner, Ralph Linton, Margaret Mead.

70. See studies of the institution of European folklore traditions from the end of the eighteenth century in their relation to romanticism, for example, the brothers Grimm and Vuk Karadic (Serbian folktales).

71. This was, briefly stated, Lucien Lévy-Bruhl's thesis in *La Mentalité primitive* (Paris: Alcan, 1922) [Eng. trans. Lillian Clare, *Primitive Mentality* (New York: Macmillan, 1923)].

72. Claude Lévi-Strauss, *La Pensée sauvage* (Paris: Plon, 1962) [Eng. trans. *The Savage Mind* (Chicago, University of Chicago, 1966)].

73. Robert Jaulin, *La paix blanche* (Paris: Seuil, 1970).

74. Vladimir Propp, *Morphology of the Folktale,* trans. Laurence Scott with intro. by Suatana Pirkora-Jakobson [Publications of the American Folklore Society, Bibliographical and Special Series, no. 9 (Bloomington, Ind., 1958); 2d ed. rev. (Austin, Tex. University of Texas Press, 1968).

75. Claude Lévi-Strauss, "La Structure des Mythes" (1955), in *Anthropologie Structurale* (Paris: Plon, 1958) [Eng. trans. Claire Jacobson and Brooke Grundfest Schoepf, *Structural Anthropology* (New York: Basic Books, 1963)], and "La Structure et la forme: Réflexions sur un ouvrage de Vladimir Propp, *Cahiers de l'Institut de science économique appliquée,* 99, series M, 7 (1960) [in Claude Lévi-Strauss, *Structural Anthropology II,* trans. Monique Layton (New York: Basic Books, 1976). The essay will also be included in Vladimir Propp, *Theory and History of Folklore,* trans. Ariadna and Richard Martin, intro. by Anatoly Liberman, Theory and History of Literature, vol. 5 (Minneapolis: University of Minnesota Press, forthcoming)].

76. Geza Róheim, *Psychoanalysis and Anthropology* (New York: International Universities Press, 1959).

77. André M. d'Ans, *Le Dit des vrais hommes* (Paris: Union Générale d'Edition, 1978).

78. Ibid., p. 7.

79. I have made use of it here because of the pragmatic "etiquette" surrounding the transmission of the narratives; the anthropologist details it with great care. See Pierre Clastres, *Le grand Parler: Mythes et chants sacrés des Indiens Guarani* (Paris: Seuil, 1972).

80. For a narratology that treats the pragmatic dimension, see Gérard Genette, *Figures III* (Paris: Seuil, 1972) [Eng. trans. Jane E. Lewin, *Narrative Discourse* (New York: Cornell University Press, 1980).

81. See note 34.

82. The relationship between meter and accent, which constitutes and dissolves rhythm, is at the center of Hegel's reflection on speculation. See sec. 4 of the preface to the *Phenomenology of Spirit*.

83. I would like to thank André M. d'Ans for kindly providing this information.

84. See Daniel Charles's analyses in *Le Temps de la voix* (Paris: Delarge, 1978) and those of Dominique Avron in *L'Appareil musical* (Paris: Union Générale d'Edition, 1978).

85. See Mircea Eliade, *Le Mythe de l'éternel retour: Archétypes et répétitions* (Paris: Gallimard, 1949) [Eng. trans. Willard R. Trask, *The Myth of the Eternal Return* (New York: Pantheon Books, 1954)].

86. The example is borrowed from Frege, "Über Sinn und Bedeutung" (1892) [Eng. trans. Max Black and Peter Geach, "On Sense and Reference," in *Translations from the Philosophical Writings of Gottlob Frege* (Oxford: Blackwell, 1960)].

87. Bruno Latour and Paolo Fabbri, "Rhétorique de la science," *Actes de la recherche en sciences sociales* 13 (1977): 81-95.

88. Gaston Bachelard, *Le Nouvel Esprit scientifique* (Paris: Presses Universitaires de France, 1934).

89. Descartes, *Méditations métaphysiques* (1641), Méditation 4.

90. See for example Karl G. Hempel, *Philosophy of Natural Science* (Englewood Cliffs, N.J.: Prentice-Hall, 1966).

91. There is no space here to discuss the difficulties raised by this double presupposition. See Vincent Descombes, *L'Inconscient malgré lui* (Paris: Editions de Minuit, 1977).

92. This remark avoids a major difficulty, one that would also arise in the examination of narration: the distinction between language games and discursive games. I will not discuss it here.

93. In the sense indicated in note 90.

94. Thomas Kuhn, *The Structure of Scientific Revolutions* (Chicago: University of Chicago Press, 1962).

95. Cf. children's attitude toward their first science lessons, or the way natives interpret the ethnologist's explanations (see Lévi-Strauss, *The Savage Mind* [note 72], chap. 1).

96. That is why Métraux commented to Clastres, "To be able to study a primitive society, it already has to be a little decayed." In effect, the native informant must be able to see his own society through the eyes of the ethnologist; he must be able to question the functioning of its institutions and therefore their legitimacy. Reflecting on his failure with the Achè tribe, Clastres concludes, "And so the Achè accepted presents they had not asked for while at the same time refusing attempts at a dialogue, because they were strong enough not to need it: we would start talking when they were sick" [quoted by M. Cartry in "Pierre Clastres," *Libre* 4 (1978)].

97. On scientistic ideology, see *Survivre* 9 (1971), reprinted in Jaubert and Lévy-Leblond, *(Auto)critique* (note 26), pp. 51ff. At the end of their collection there is a bibliography listing periodicals and groups fighting against the various forms of subordination of science to the system.

98. Victor Goldschmidt, *Les Dialogues de Platon* (Paris: Presses Universitaires de France, 1947).

99. These terms are borrowed from Genette, *Figures III*.

100. Paul Valéry, *Introduction à la méthode de Léonard de Vinci* (1894) [(Paris: Galli-mard, 1957): this volume also contains "Marginalia" (1930), "Note et digression" (1919), "Léonard et les philosophes" (1929); Eng. trans. in *The Collected Works of Paul Valéry*, ed. Jackson Matthews (Princeton: Princeton University Press, 1956-75), vol. 8].

101. Pierre Aubenque, *Le Problème de l'Etre chez Aristote* (Paris: Presses Universitaires de France, 1962).

102. Pierre Duhem, *Essai sur la notion de théorie physique de Platon à Galilée* (Paris: Hermann, 1908) [Eng. trans. Edmund Doland and Chaninah Maschler, *To Save the Phenomena: An Essay in the Idea of Physical Theory from Plato to Galileo* (Chicago: University of Chicago Press, 1969)]; Alexandre Koyré, *Etudes Galiléennes* (1940; Paris: Hermann, 1966 [Eng. trans. John Mephan, *Galileo Studies* (Hassocks, Eng.: Harvester Press, 1978)]; Thomas Kuhn, *Structure of Scientific Revolutions*.

103. Michel de Certeau, Dominique Julia, Jacques Revel, *Une Politique de la langue: La Révolution Française et les patois* (Paris: Gallimard, 1975).

104. On the distinction between prescriptions and norms, see G. Kalinowski, "Du Méta-language en logique. Réflexions sur la logique déontique et son rapport avec la logique des normes," *Documents de travail* 48 (Università di Urbino, 1975).

105. A trace of this politics is to be found in the French institution of a philosophy class at the end of secondary studies, and in the proposal by the Groupe de recherches sur l'en-seignement de la philosophie (GREPH) to teach "some" philosophy starting at the beginning of secondary studies: see their *Qui a peur de la philosophie?* (Paris: Flammarion, 1977), sec. 2, "La Philosophie déclassée." This also seems to be the orientation of the curriculum of the CEGEP's in Quebec, especially of the philosophy courses (see for example the *Cahiers de l'enseignement collégial* (1975-76) for philosophy).

106. See H. Janne, "L'Université et les besoins de la société contemporaine," *Cahiers de l'Association internationale des Universités* 10 (1970) 5, quoted by the Commission d'étude sur les universités, *Document de consultation* (Montréal, 1978).

107. A "hard," almost mystico-military expression of this can be found in Julio de Mesquita Filho, *Discorso de Paraninfo da primeiro turma de licenciados pela Faculdade de Filosofia, Ciências e Letras da Universidade de Saô Paulo* (25 January 1937), and an expression of it adapted to the modern problems of Brazilian development in the *Relatorio do Grupo de Rabalho, Reforma Universitaria* (Brasilia: Ministries of Education and Culture, etc., 1968). These documents are part of a dossier on the university in Brazil, kindly sent to me by Helena C. Chamlian and Martha Ramos de Carvalho of the University of São Paulo.

108. The documents are available in French thanks to Miguel Abensour and the Collège de philosophie: *Philosophes de l'Université: L'Idéalisme allemand et la question de l'université* (Paris: Payot, 1979). The collection includes texts by Schelling, Fichte, Schleiermacher, Humboldt, and Hegel.

109. "Über die innere und äussere Organisation der höheren wissenschaftlichen Anstalten in Berlin" (1810), in *Wilhelm von Humboldt* (Frankfurt, 1957), p. 126.

110. Ibid., p. 128.

111. Friedrich Schleiermacher, "Gelegentliche Gedanken über Universitäten in deutschen Sinn, nebst einem Anhang über eine neu zu errichtende" (1808), in E. Spranger, ed., *Fichte, Schleiermacher, Steffens über das Wesen der Universität* (Leipzig, 1910), p. 126ff.

112. "The teaching of philosophy is generally recognized to be the basis of all university activity" (ibid., p. 128).

113. Alain Touraine has analyzed the contradictions involved in this transplantation in *Université et société aux Etats-Unis* (Paris: Seuil, 1972), pp. 32-40 [Eng. trans. *The Academic System in American Society* (New York: McGraw-Hill, 1974)].

114. It is present even in the conclusions of Robert Nisbet, *The Degradation of the*

Academic Dogma: The University in America, 1945-70 (London: Heinemann, 1971). The author is a professor at the University of California, Riverside.

115. See G. W. F. Hegel, *Philosophie des Rechts* (1821) [Eng. trans. T. M. Knox, *Hegel's Philosophy of Right* (Oxford: Oxford University Press, 1967)].

116. See Paul Ricoeur, *Le Conflit des interprétations. Essais d'herméneutique* (Paris: Seuil, 1969) [Eng. trans. Don Ihde, *The Conflict of Interpretations* (Evanston, Ill.: Northwestern University Press, 1974)]; Hans Georg Gadamer, *Warheit und Methode* 2d ed. (Tübingen: Mohr, 1965) [Eng. trans. Garrett Barden and John Cumming, *Truth and Method* (New York: Seabury Press, 1975)].

117. Take two statements: 1) "The moon has risen"; 2) "The statement /The moon has risen/ is a denotative statement". The syntagm /The moon has risen/ in statement 2 is said to be the autonym of statement 1. See Josette Rey-Debove, *Le Métalangage* (Paris: Le Robert, 1978), pt. 4.

118. Its principle is Kantian, at least in matters of transcendental ethics—see the *Critique of Practical Reason*. When it comes to politics and empirical ethics, Kant is prudent: since no one can identify himself with the transcendental normative subject, it is theoretically more exact to compromise with the existing authorities. See for example, "Antwort an der Frage: 'Was ist "Aufklärung"?' " (1784) [Eng. trans. Lewis White Beck, in *Critique of Practical Reason and Other Writings in Moral Philosophy* (Chicago: Chicago University Press, 1949)].

119. See Kant, "Antwort"; Jürgen Habermas, *Strukturwandel der Öffentlichkeit* (Frankfort: Luchterhand, 1962). The principle of *Öffentlichkeit* ("public" or "publicity" in the sense of "making public a private correspondence" or "public debate") guided the action of many groups of scientists at the end of the 1960s, especially the group "Survivre" (France), the group "Scientists and Engineers for Social and Political Action" (USA), and the group "British Society for Social Responsibility in Science."

120. A French translation of this text by G. Granel can be found in *Phi*, supplement to the *Annales de l'université de Toulouse—Le Mirail* (Toulouse: January 1977).

121. See note 1. Certain scientific aspects of postmodernism are inventoried by Ihab Hassan in "Culture, Indeterminacy, and Immanence: Margins of the (Postmodern) Age," *Humanities in Society* 1 (1978): 51-85.

122. Claus Mueller uses the expression "a process of delegitimation" in *The Politics of Communication* (New York: Oxford University Press, 1973), p. 164.

123. "Road of doubt . . . road of despair . . skepticism," writes Hegel in the preface to the *Phenomenology of Spirit* to describe the effect of the speculative drive on natural knowledge.

124. For fear of encumbering this account, I have postponed until a later study the exposition of this group of rules. [See "Analyzing Speculative Discourse as Language-Game," *The Oxford Literary Review* 4, no. 3 (1981): 59-67.]

125. Nietzsche, "Der europäische Nihilismus" (MS. N VII 3); "der Nihilism, ein normaler Zustand" (MS. W II 1); "Kritik der Nihilism" (MS. W VII 3); "Zum Plane" (MS. W II 1), in *Nietzshes Werke kritische Gesamtausgabe*, vol. 7, pts. 1 and 2 (1887-89) (Berlin: De Gruyter, 1970). These texts have been the object of a commentary by K. Ryjik, *Nietzsche, le manuscrit de Lenzer Heide* (typescript, Département de philosophie, Université de Paris VIII [Vincennes]).

126. "On the future of our educational institutions," in *Complete Works* (note 35), vol. 3.

127. Martin Buber, *Ich und Du* (Berlin: Schocken Verlag, 1922) [Eng. trans. Ronald G. Smith, *I and Thou* (New York: Charles Scribner's Sons, 1937)], and *Dialogisches Leben* (Zürich: Müller, 1947); Emmanuel Lévinas, *Totalité et Infinité* (La Haye: Nijhoff, 1961) [Eng. trans. Alphonso Lingis, *Totality and Infinity: An Essay on Exteriority* (Pittsburgh:

Duquesne University Press, 1969)], and "Martin Buber und die Erkenntnis theorie" (1958), in *Philosophen des 20. Jahrhunderts* (Stuttgart: Kohlhammer, 1963) [Fr. trans. "Martin Buber et la théorie de la connaissance," in *Noms Propres* (Montpellier: Fata Morgana, 1976)].

128. *Philosophical Investigations*, sec. 18, p. 8.

129. Ibid.

130. Ibid.

131. See for example, "La taylorisation de la recherche," in *(Auto)critique de la science* (note 26), pp. 291-93. And especially D. J. de Solla Price, *Little Science, Big Science* (New York: Columbia University Press, 1963), who emphasizes the split between a small number of highly productive researchers (evaluated in terms of publication) and a large mass of researchers with low productivity. The number of the latter grows as the square of the former, so that the number of high productivity researchers only really increases every twenty years. Price concludes that science considered as a social entity is "undemocratic" (p. 59) and that "the eminent scientist" is a hundred years ahead of "the minimal one" (p. 56).

132. See J. T. Desanti, "Sur le rapport traditionnel des sciences et de la philosophie," in *La Philosophie silencieuse, ou critique des philosophies de la science* (Paris: Seuil, 1975).

133. The reclassification of academic philosophy as one of the human sciences in this respect has a significant far beyond simply professional concerns. I do not think that philosophy as legitimation is condemned to disappear, but it is possible that it will not be able to carry out this work, or at least advance it, without revising its ties to the university institution. See on this matter the preamble to the *Projet d'un institut polytechnique de philosophie* (typescript, Département de philosophie, Université de Paris VIII [Vincennes], 1979).

134. See Allan Janik and Stephan Toulmin, *Wittgenstein's Vienna* (New York: Simon & Schuster, 1973), and J. Piel, ed., "Vienne début d'un siècle," *Critique*, 339-40 (1975).

135. See Jürgen Habermas, "Dogmatismus, Vernunft unt Entscheidung—Zu Theorie und Praxis in der verwissenschaftlichen Zivilisation" (1963), in *Theorie und Praxis* [*Theory and Practice*, abr. ed. of 4th German ed., trans. John Viertel (Boston: Beacon Press, 1971)].

136. "Science Smiling Into its Beard" is the title of chap. 72, vol. 1 of Musil's *The Man Without Qualities*. Cited and discussed by J. Bouveresse, "La Problématique du sujet" (note 54).

137. Aristotle in the *Analytics* (ca. 330 B.C.), Descartes in the *Regulae ad directionem ingenii* (1641) and the *Principes de la philosophie* (1644), John Stuart Mill in the *System of Logic* (1843).

138. Gaston Bachelard, *Le Rationalisme appliqué* (Paris: Presses Universitaires de France, 1949); Michel Serres, "La Réforme et les sept péchés," *L'Arc* 42, Bachelard special issue (1970).

139. David Hilbert, *Grundlagen der Geometrie* (1899) [Eng. trans. Leo Unger, *Foundations of Geometry* (La Salle: Open Court, 1971)]. Nicolas Bourbaki, "L'architecture des mathématiques," in Le Lionnais, ed., *Les Grands Courants de la pensée mathématique* (Paris: Hermann, 1948); Robert Blanché, *L'Axiomatique* (Paris: Presses Universitaires de France, 1955) [Eng. trans. G. B. Keene, *Axiomatics* (New York: Free Press of Glencoe, 1962)].

140. See Blanché, *L'Axiomatique*, chap. 5.

141. I am here following Robert Martin, *Logique contemporaine et formalisation* (Paris: Presses Universitaires de France, 1964), pp. 33-41 and 122ff.

142. Kurt Gödel, "Über formal unentscheidbare Sätze der Principia Mathematica und verwandter Systeme," *Monatshefte für Mathematik und Physik* 38 (1931) [Eng. trans. B. Bletzer, *On Formally Undecidable Propositions of Principia Mathematica and Related Systems* (New York: Basic Books, 1962)].

143. Jean Ladrière, *Les Limitations internes des formalismes* (Louvain: E. Nauwelaerts, 1957).

144. Alfred Tarski, *Logic, Semantics, Metamathematics*, trans. J. H. Woodger (Oxford: Clarendon Press, 1956); J. P. Desclès and Z. Guentcheva-Desclès, "Métalangue, métalangage, métalinguistique," *Documents de travail* 60-61 (Università di Urbino, January-February 1977).

145. *Les Eléments des mathématiques* (Paris: Hermann, 1940-   ). The distant points of departure of this work are to be found in the first attempts to demonstrate certain "postulates" of Euclidian geometry. See Léon Brunschvicg, *Les Etapes de la philosophie mathématique*, 3d ed. (Paris: Presses Universitaires de France, 1947).

146. Thomas Kuhn, *Structure of Scientific Revolutions* (note 94).

147. A classification of logico-mathematical paradoxes can be found in F. P. Ramsey, *The Foundations of Mathematics and Other Logical Essays* (New York: Harcourt & Brace, 1931).

148. See Aristotle, *Rhetoric* 2. 1393a ff.

149. The problem is that of the witness and also of the historical source: is the fact known from hearsay or *de visu?* The distinction is made by Herodotus. See F. Hartog, "Hérodote rapsode et arpenteur," *Hérodote* 9 (1977): 55-65.

150. A. Gehlen, "Die Technik in der Sichtweise der Anthropologie," *Anthropologische Forschung* (Hamburg: Rowohlt, 1961).

151. André Leroi-Gourhan, *Milieu et techniques* (Paris: Albin-Michel, 1945), and *Le Geste et la parole, I, Technique et langage* (Paris: Albin-Michel, 1964).

152. Jean Pierre Vernant, *Mythe et pensée chez les Grecs* (Paris: Maspero, 1965), especially sec. 4, "Le travail et la pensée technique" [Eng. trans. Janet Lloyd, *Myth and Society in Ancient Greece* (Brighton, Eng.: Harvester Press, 1980)].

153. Jurgis Baltrusaitis, *Anamorphoses, ou magie artificielle des effets merveilleux* (Paris: O. Perrin, 1969) [Eng. trans. W. J. Strachan, *Anamorphic Art* (New York: Abrams, 1977)].

154. Lewis Mumford, *Technics and Civilization* New York: Harcourt, Brace, 1963); Bertrand Gille, *Historie des Techniques* (Paris: Gallimard, Pléiade, 1978).

155. A striking example of this, the use of amateur radios to verify certain implications of the theory of relativity, is studied by M. J. Mulkay and D. O. Edge, "Cognitive, Technical, and Social Factors in the Growth of Radio-Astronomy," *Social Science Information* 12, no. 6 (1973): 25-61.

156. Mulkay elaborates a flexible model for the relative independence of technology and scientific knowledge in "The Model of Branching," *The Sociological Review* 33 (1976): 509-26. H. Brooks, president of the Science and Public Committee of the National Academy of Sciences, and coauthor of the "Brooks Report" (OCDE, June 1971), criticizing the method of investment in research and development during the 1960s, declares: "One of the effects of the race to the moon has been to increase the cost of technological innovation to the point where it becomes quite simply too expensive. . . . Research is properly speaking a long-term activity: rapid acceleration or deceleration imply concealed expenditure and a great deal of incompetence. Intellectual production cannot go beyond a certain pace" ("Les Etats-Unis ont-ils une politique de la science?" *La Recherche* 14 [1971]: 611). In March 1972, E. E. David, Jr., scientific adviser to the White House, proposing the idea of a program of Research Applied to National Needs (RANN), came to similar conclusions: a broad and flexible strategy for research and more restrictive tactics for development (*La Recherche* 21 (1972): 211).

157. This was one of the Lazarsfeld's conditions for agreeing to found what was to become the Mass Communication Research Center at Princeton in 1937. This produced some tension: the radio industries refused to invest in the project; people said that Lazarsfeld started things going but finished nothing. Lazarsfeld himself said to Morrison, "I usually put things together and hoped they worked." Quoted by D. Morrison, "The Beginning of Modern Mass Communication Research," *Archives européennes de sociologie* 19, no. 2 (1978): 347-59.

158. In the United States, the funds allocated to research and development by the federal government were, in 1956, equal to the funds coming from private capital; they have been higher since that time (OCDE, 1956).

159. Robert Nisbet, *Degradation* (note 114), chap. 5, provides a bitter description of the penetration of "higher capitalism" into the university in the form of research centers independent of departments. The social relations in such centers disturb the academic tradition. See too in *(Auto)critique de la science* (note 26), the chapters "Le prolétariat scientifique," "Les chercheurs," "La Crise des mandarins."

160. Niklas Luhmann, *Legitimation durch Verfahren* (Neuweid: Luchterhand, 1969).

161. Commenting on Luhmann, Mueller writes, "In advanced industrial society, legal-rational legitimation is replaced by a technocratic legitimation that does not accord any significance to the beliefs of the citizen or to morality per se" *(Politics of Communication* [note 122], p. 135). There is a bibliography of German material on the technocratic question in Habermas, *Theory and Practice* (note 39).

162. Gilles Fauconnier gives a linguistic analysis of the control of truth in "Comment contrôler la vérité? Remarques illustrées par des assertions dangereuses et pernicieuses en tout genre," *Actes de la recherche en sciences sociales* 25 (1979): 1-22.

163. Thus in 1970 the British University Grants Committee was "persuaded to take a much more positive role in productivity, specialization, concentration of subjects, and control of building through cost limits" [*The Politics of Education: Edward Boyle and Anthony Crosland in Conversation with Maurice Kogan* (Harmondsworth, Eng.: Penguin, 1971), p. 196]. This may appear to contradict declarations such as that of Brooks, quoted above (note 156). But 1) the "strategy" may be liberal and the "tactics" authoritarian, as Edwards says elsewhere; 2) responsibility within the hierarchy of public authorities is often taken in its narrowest sense, namely the capacity to answer for the calculable performance of a project; 3) public authorities are not always free from pressures from private groups whose performance criterion is immediately binding. If the chances of innovation in research cannot be calculated, then public interest seems to lie in aiding all research, under conditions other than that of efficiency assessment after a fixed period.

164. During the seminars run by Lazarsfeld at the Princeton Radio Research Center in 1939-40, Laswell defined the process of communication in the formula, "Who says what to whom in what channel with what effect?" see D. Morrison, "Beginning."

165. This is what Parsons defines as "instrumental activism" and glorifies to the point of confusing it with "cognitive rationality": "The orientation of cognitive rationality is implicit in the common culture of instrumental activism but it only becomes more or less explicit and is more highly appreciated among the educated classes and the intellectuals by whom it is more evidently applied in their occupational pursuits" [Talcott Parsons and Gerald M. Platt, "Considerations on the American Academic Systems," *Minerva* 6 (Summer 1968): 507; cited by Alain Touraine, *Université et société* (note 113), p. 146].

166. What Mueller terms the *professional intelligentsia*, as opposed to the *technical intelligentsia*. Following John Kenneth Galbraith, he describes the alarm and resistance of the professional intelligentsia in the face of technocratic legitimation (*Politics of Communication* [note 122], pp. 172-77).

167. At the beginning of the academic year 1970-71, 30-40% of 19-year-olds were registered in higher education in Canada, the United States, the USSR, and Yugoslavia, and about 20% in Germany, France, Great Britain, Japan, and the Netherlands. In all of these countries, the number had doubled or tripled since 1959. According to the same source (M. Devèze, *Histoire contemporaine de l'université* (Paris: SEDES, 1976), pp. 439-40), the proportion of students in the total population had increased from about 4% to about 10% in Western Europe, from 6.1% to 21.3% in Canada, and from 15.1% to 32.5% for the United States.

168. In France, the total higher education budget (not counting the CNRS) increased from 3,075 million francs in 1968 to 5,454 million in 1975, representing a decrease from about 0.55% to 0.39% of the GNP. Increases in absolute figures came in the areas of salaries, operating expenses, and scholarships; the amount for research subsidies remained more or less the same (Devèze, *Histoire*, pp. 447-50). E. E. David states that the demand for Ph.D.'s in the 1970 was scarcely higher than in the 1960s (p. 212 [see note 156]).

169. In Mueller's terminology, *Politics of Communication* (note 122).

170. This is what J. Dofny and M. Rioux discuss under the rubric "cultural training." See "Inventaire et bilan de quelques expériences d'intervention de l'universite," in *L'Université dans son milieu: action et responsabilité* (AUPELF conference, Université de Montréal, 1971), pp. 155-62). The authors criticize what they call the two types of Northern American universities: the liberal arts colleges, in which teaching and research are entirely divorced from social demand, and the "multiversity," which is willing to dispense any teaching the community is prepared to pay for. On this last system, see Clark Kerr, *The Uses of the University: With a Postscript – 1972* (Cambridge, Mass., Harvard University Press, 1972). Moving in a similar direction, but without the interventionism of the university in society recommended by Dofny and Rioux, see the description of the university of the future given by M. Alliot during the same conference: "Structures optimales de l'institution universitaire," ibid., pp. 141-54. M. Alliot concludes: "We believe in structures, when there really ought to be as few structures as possible." This was the goal of the Centre expérimental, subsequently Université de Paris VIII (Vincennes), as declared at its founding in 1968. See for this, the dossier *Vincennes ou le désir d'apprendre* (Paris: Alain-Moreau, 1979).

171. It is the author's personal experience that this was the case with a large number of departments at Vincennes.

172. The higher education reform law of November 12, 1968, numbers continuing education (conceived in a professionalistic sense) among the duties of higher education, which "should be open to former students and to those who have not been able to study, in order to allow them to increase their chances of promotion or change occupations, according to their abilities."

173. In an interview with *Télé-sept-jours* 981 (17 March 1979), the French minister of Education, who had officially recommended the series *Holocaust* broadcast on Channel 2 to public school students (an unprecedented step), declared that the education sector's attempt to create for itself an autonomous audiovisual tool has failed and that "the first task of education is to teach children how to choose their programs" on television.

174. In Great Britain, where the State's contribution to the capital outlays and operating expenses of the universities increased from 30% to 80% between 1920 and 1960, it is the University Grants Committee, attached to the Ministry of State for Science and Universities, which distributes the annual subsidy after studying the needs and development plans presented by the universities. In the United States the trustees are all-powerful.

175. In France, that means distributing among the departments the funds earmarked for operating expenses and equipment. Instructors only have power over salaries in the case of temporary personnel. Financing for projects and administrative reorganization, etc., is taken from the overall teaching budget allocated to the university.

176. Marshall McLuhan, *Essays* (Montreal: Hartubise Ltd., 1977); P. Antoine, "Comment s'informer?" *Projet* 124 (1978): 395-413.

177. It is well known that the use of intelligent terminals is taught to school children in Japan. In Canada they are used regularly by isolated university and college departments.

178. This policy has been pursued by American research centers since before the Second World War.

179. Nora and Minc (*L'Informatisation de la société* [note 9], p. 16) write: "The major challenge for the advanced poles of humanity in the coming decades is no longer that of

mastering matter—such mastery is already assured. The challenge is rather that of constructing a network of links allowing information and orgaization to move forward together."

180. Anatol Rapoport, *Fights, Games, and Debates* (Ann Arbor: University of Michigan Press, 1960).

181. This is Mulkay's Branching Model (see note 156). Gilles Deleuze has analyzed events in terms of the intersection of series in *Logique du sens* (Paris: Editions de Minuit, 1969) and *Différence et répétition* (Paris: Presses Universitaires de France, 1968).

182. Time is a variable in the determination of the power factor in dynamics. See also Paul Virilio, *Vitesse et politique* (Paris: Galilee, 1976) [Eng. trans. *Speed and Politics* (New York: Semiotexte, forthcoming)].

183. Jacob L. Moreno, *Who shall survive?* rev. ed. (Beacon, N.Y.: Beacon House, 1953).

184. Among the best known are: the Mass Communication Research Center (Princeton); the Mental Research Institute (Palo Alto); the Massachusetts Institute of Technology (Boston); Institut für Sozialforschung (Frankfurt). Part of Clark Kerr's argument in favor of what he calls the Ideapolis is based on the principle that collective research increases inventiveness (*Uses of the University*, pp. 91ff.).

185. Solla Price, *Little Science, Big Science* (note 131), attempts to found a science of science. He establishes the (statistical) laws of science as a social object. I have already referred to the law of undemocratic division in note 131. Another law, that of "invisible colleges," describes the effect of the increasing number of publications and the saturation of information channels in scientific institutions: the "aristocrats" of knowledge are tending to react to this by setting up stable networks of interpersonal contact involving at most about a hundred selected members. Diana Crane has provided a sociometric analysis of these colleges in *Invisible Colleges* (Chicago and London: University of Chicago Press, 1972). See Lécuyer, "Bilan et perspectives" (note 24).

186. In *Fractals: Form, Chance and Dimension* (San Francisco: W. H. Freeman, 1977), Benoit Mandelbrot provides an appendix of "Biographical and Historical Sketches" (pp. 249-73) of researchers in mathematics and physics who were recognized late or not at all, despite the fecundity of their research, because their interests were unusual.

187. A famous example of this is the debate on determinism occasioned by quantum mechanics. See for example J. M. Lévy-Leblond's presentation of the Born-Einstein correspondence (1916-55), "Le grand débat de la mécanique quantique," *La Recherche* 20 (1972): 137-44. The history of the human sciences in the last century is full of such shifts from anthropological discourse to the level of metalanguage.

188. Ihab Hassan gives an "image" of what he terms *immanence* in "Culture, Indeterminacy, and Immanence" (note 121).

189. See note 142.

190. Pierre Simon Laplace, *Exposition du système du monde*, 2 vols. (1796) [Eng. trans. Henry Harte, *The System of the World*, 2 vols. (Dublin: Dublin University Press, 1830)].

191. "Del Rigor en la ciencia," in *Historia Universal de la Infamia*, 2d. ed. (Buenos Aires: Emecé, 1954), pp. 131-32. [Eng. trans. N. T. di Giovanni, *A Universal History of Infamy* (New York: Dutton, 1972)].

192. Information itself costs energy, and the negentropy it constitutes gives rise to entropy. Michel Serres often refers to this argument, for example, in *Hermès III: La Traduction* (Paris: Editions de Minuit, 1974), p. 92.

193. I follow Ilya Prigogine and I. Stengers, "La Dynamique, de Leibniz à Lucrèce," *Critique* 380, Serres special issue (1979): 49.

194. Jean Baptiste Perrin, *Less Atomes* (1913; Paris: Presses Universitaires de France, 1970), pp. 14-22. The text is used by Mendelbrot as an introduction to *Fractals*.

195. Quoted by Werner Heisenberg, *Physics and Beyond* (New York: Harper & Row, 1971).

196. In a paper presented to the Académie des sciences (December 1921), Borel suggested that "in games in which the best way to play does not exist" (games without perfect information), "one might wonder whether, in the absence of a code chosen once and for all, it might be possible to play advantageously by varying one's game." It is on the basis of this distinction that von Neumann shows that this probabilization of the decision is itself, in certain conditions, "the best way to play." See Georges Guilbaud, *Eléments de la théorie mathématique des jeux* (Paris: Dunod, 1968), pp. 17-21, and J. P. Séris, *La Théorie des jeux* (Paris: Presses Universitaires de France, 1974) (collection of texts). "Postmodern" artists use these concepts frequently; see for example John Cage, *Silence* and *A Year From Monday* (Middletown, Conn.: Wesleyan University Press, 1961 and 1967).

197. I. Epstein, "Jogos" (typescript, Fundaçaô Armando Alvares Penteado, September 1978).

198. "Probability reappears here, no longer as the constitutive principle of the structure of an object, but as the regulating principle of a structure of behavior" (Gilles-Gaston Granger, *Pensée formelle et sciences de l'homme* [Paris: Aubier-Montaigne, 1960] , p. 142). The idea that the gods play bridge, say, would be more like a pre-Platonic Greek hypothesis.

199. Mandelbrot, *Fractals*, p. 5.

200. A continuous nonrectifiable, self-similar curve, described by Mandelbrot, pp. 38ff., and established by H. von Koch in 1904: see the bibliography to *Fractals*.

201. *Modèles mathématiques de la morphogenèse* (note 14). An account of catastrophe theory accessible to the layman is provided by K. Pomian, "Catastrophes et déterminisme," *Libre* 4 (1978): 115-36.

202. Pomian borrows this example from E. C. Zeeman, "The Geometry of Catastrophe," *The Times Literary Supplement,* 10 December 1971.

203. René Thom, *Stabilité structurelle et morphogenèse: Essai d'une théorie générale des modèles* (Reading, Mass.: W. A. Benjamin, 1972), p. 25 [Eng. trans. D. M. Fowler, *Structural Stability and Morphogenesis* (Reading, Mass.: W. A. Benjamin, 1975)] . Quoted by Pomian, "Catastrophes." p. 134.

204. René Thom, *Modèles mathématiques,* p. 24.

205. Ibid., p. 25.

206. See especially Watzlawick et al., *Pragmatics of Human Communication* (note 11), chap. 6.

207. "The conditions of production of scientific knowledge must be distinguished from the knowledge produced. . . . There are two constitutive stages of scientific activity: making the known unknown, and then reorganizing this unknowledge into an independent symbolic metasystem. . . . The specificity of science is in its unpredictability" (P. Breton, in *Pandore* 3 (1979): 10).

208. Anatol Rapoport, *Two-Person Game Theory* (Ann Arbor: University of Michigan Press, 1966), p. 202.

209. P. B. Medawar, *The Art of the Soluble,* 6th ed. (London: Methuen, 1967), p. 116; and see especially the chapters entitled "Two Conceptions of Science" and "Hypothesis and Imagination."

210. This is explained by Paul Feyerabend, *Against Method* (London: New Left Books, 1975), using the example of Galileo. Feyerabend champions epistemological "anarchism" or "dadaism" in opposition to Popper and Lakatos.

211. It has not been possible within the limits of this study to analyze the form assumed by the return of narrative in discourses of legitimation. Examples are: the study of open systems, local determinism, antimethod—in general, everything that I group under the name *paralogy*.

212. Nora and Minc, for example, attribute Japan's success in the field of computers to an "intensity of social consensus" that they judge to be specific to Japanese society

(*L'Informatisation de la Société* [note 9], p. 4). They write in their conclusion: "The dynamics of extended social computerization leads to a fragile society: such a society is constructed with a view to facilitating consensus, but already presupposes its existence, and comes to a standstill if that consensus cannot be realized" (p. 125). Y. Stourdzé, "Les Etats-Unis" (note 20), emphasizes the fact that the current tendency to deregulate, destabilize, and weaken administration is encouraged by society's loss of confidence in the State's performance capability.

213. In Kuhn's sense.

214. Pomian ("Catastrophes") shows that this type of functioning bears no relation to Hegelian dialectics.

215. "What the legitimation of decisions accordingly entails is fundamentally an effective learning process, with a minimum of friction, within the social system. This is an aspect of the more general question, "how do aspirations change, how can the political-administrative subsystem, itself only part of society, nevertheless structure expectations in society through its decisions?' The effectiveness of the activity of what is only a part, for the whole, will in large measure depend on how well it succeeds in integrating new expectations into already existing systems—whether these are persons or social systems—without thereby provoking considerable functional disturbances" (Niklas Luhmann, *Legitimation durch Verfahren* [note 160] , p. 35).

216. This hypothesis is developed in David Riesman's earlier studies. See Riesman, *The Lonely Crowd* (New Haven: Yale University Press, 1950); W. H. Whyte, *The Organization Man* (New York: Simon & Schuster, 1956); Herbert Marcuse, *One Dimensional Man* (Boston: Beacon, 1966).

217. Josette Rey-Debove (*Le Métalangage* [note 117], pp. 228ff ` notes the proliferation of marks of indirect discourse or autonymic connotation in contemporary daily language. As she reminds us, "indirect discourse cannot be trusted "

218. As Georges Canguilhem says, "man is only truly healthy when he is capable of a number of norms, when he is more than normal" ("Le Normal et la pathologique" [1951] , in *La Connaissance de la vie* [Paris: Hachette, 1952], p. 210) [Eng. trans. Carolyn Fawcett, *On the Normal and the Pathological* (Boston: D. Reidel, 1978)] .

219. E. E. David (note 156) comments that society can only be aware of the needs it feels in the present state of its technological milieu. It is of the nature of the basic sciences to discover unknown properties which remodel the technical milieu and create unpredictable needs. He cites as examples the use of solid materials as amplifiers and the rapid development of the physics of solids. This "negative regulation" of social interactions and needs by the object of contemporary techniques is critiqued by R. Jaulin, "Le Mythe technologique," *Revue de l'entreprise* 26, special "Ethnotechnology" issue (March 1979): 49-55. This is a review of A. G. Haudricourt, "La Technologie culturelle, essai de méthodologie," in Gille, *Historie des techniques* (note 154).

220. Medawar (*Art of the Soluble*, pp. 151-52) compares scientists' written and spoken styles. The former must be "inductive" or they will not be considered; as for the second, Medawar makes a list of expressions often heard in laboratories, including, "My results don't make a story yet." He concludes, "Scientists are building explanatory structures, *telling stories.* . . . "

221. For a famous example, see Lewis S. Feuer, *Einstein and the Generations of Science* (New York: Basic Books, 1974). As Moscovici emphasizes in his introduction to the French translation [trans. Alexandre, *Einstein et le conflit des générations* (Bruxelles' Complexe, 1979)] , "Relativity was born in a makeshift 'academy' formed by friends, not one of whom was a physicist; all were engineers or amateur philosophers."

222. Orwell's paradox. The bureaucrat speaks: "We are not content with negative obedience, nor even with the most abject submission. When finally you do surrender to us, it

must be of your own free will" (*1984* [New York: Harcourt, Brace, 1949], p. 258). In language game terminology the paradox would be expressed as a "Be free," or a "Want what you want," and is analyzed by Watzlawick et al., *Pragmatics of Human Communication* (note 11), pp. 203-7. On these paradoxes, see J. M. Salanskis, "Genèses 'actuelles' et genèses 'sérielles' de l'inconsistant et de l'hétérogeme," *Critique* 379 (1978): 1155-73.

223. See Nora and Minc's description of the tensions that mass computerization will inevitably produce in French society (*L'Informatisation de la société* [note 9], introduction).

224. See note 181. Cf. the discussion of open systems in Watzlawick et al., *Pragmatics of Human Communication* (note 11), pp. 117-48. The concept of open systems theory is the subject of a study by J. M. Salanskis, *Le Systématique ouvert* (forthcoming).

225. After the separation of Church and State, Paul Feyerabend (*Against Method*), demands in the same "lay" spirit the separation of Science and State. But what about Science and Money?

226. This is at least one way of understanding this term, which comes from Ducrot's problematic, *Dire* (note 28).

227. *Legitimationsprobleme* (note 27), passim, especially pp. 21-22: "Language functions in the manner of a transformer . . . changing cognitions into propositions, needs and feelings into normative expectations (commands, values). This transformation produces the far-reaching distinction between the subjectivity of intention, willing, of pleasure and unpleasure on the one hand, and expressions and norms with a *pretension to universality* on the other. Universality signifies the objectivity of knowledge and the legitimacy of prevailing norms; both assure the community [*Gemeinsamkeit*] constitutive of lived social experience." We see that by formulating the problematic in this way, the question of legitimacy is fixated on one type of reply, universality. This on the one hand presupposes that the legitimation of the subject of knowledge is identical to that of the subject of action (in opposition to Kant's critique, which dissociates conceptual universality, appropriate to the former, and ideal universality, or "suprasensible nature," which forms the horizon of the latter, and on the other hand it maintains that consensus (*Gemeinschaft*) is the only possible horizon for the life of humanity.

228. Ibid., p. 20. The subordination of the metaprescriptives of prescription (i.e., the normalization of laws) to *Diskurs* is explicit, for example, on p. 144: "The normative pretension to validity is itself cognitive in the sense that it always assumes it could be accepted in a rational discussion."

229. Garbis Kortian, *Métacritique* (Paris: Editions de Minuit, 1979) [Eng. trans. John Raffan, *Metacritique: The Philosophical Argument of Jürgen Habermas* (Cambridge: Cambridge University Press, 1980)], pt. 5, examines this enlightenment aspect of Habermas's thought. See by the same author, "Le Discours philosphique et son objet," *Critique* 384 (1979): 407-19.

230. See J. Poulain, ("Vers une pragmatique nucléaire" [note 28]), and for a more general discussion of the pragmatics of Searle and Gehlen, see J. Poulain, "Pragmatique de la parole et pragmatique de la vie," *Phi zéro* 7, no. 1 (Université de Montréal, September 1978): 5-50.

231. See Tricot et al., *Informatique et libertés*, government report (La Documentation francaise, 1975); L. Joinet, "Les 'pièges liberaticides' de l'informatique," *Le Monde diplomatique* 300 (March 1979): these traps (*pièges*) are " the application of the technique of 'social profiles' to the management of the mass of the population; the logic of security prduced by the automatization of society." See too the documents and analysis in *Interférences* 1 and 2 (Winter 1974-Spring 1975), the theme of which is the establishment of popular networks of multimedia communication. Topics treated include: amateur radios (especially their role in Quebec during the FLQ affair of October 1970 and that of the

"Front commun" in May 1972); community radios in the United States and Canada; the impact of computers on editorial work in the press; pirate radios (before their development in Italy); administrative files, the IBM monopoly, computer sabotage. The municipality of Yverdon (Canton of Vaud), having voted to buy a computer (operational in 1981), enacted a certain number of rules: exclusive authority of the municipal council to decide which data are collected, to whom and under what conditions they are communicated; access for all citizens to all data (on payment); the right of every citizen to see the entries on his file (about 50), to correct them and address a complaint about them to the municipal council and if need be to the Council of State; the right of all citizens to know (on request) which data concerning them is communicated and to whom (*La Semaine media* 18, 1 March 1979, 9).

Index

Index

52, 53, 57, 63, 66; of perfect information, 51-52, 67; and situations, xi;
without perfect information, 57; and
performance criterion, 62; position of
the self in, 15; prescriptive, 10, 23, 36,
40, 46, 65; technical, 46. *See also* Know-
ledge, narrative and scientific
Laplace, Pierre, 55, 58
Learning. *See* Knowledge
Le Corbusier, xvii
Lefebvre, Henri, vii
Legitimation: crisis, vii, viii; and cultural im-
perialism, 27; defined, 8; language of,
38-39; by paralogy, 60-66; in post-
modernity, 37, 41; of scientific know-
ledge, 6-8, 27-31, 41-47, 54. *See also*
Knowledge, narrative
Lenin, Nikolai, xiv
Lévinas, Emmanuel, 40
Lévi-Strauss, Claude, xix
Liberalism, 6, 12, 13, 49
Lissitsky, Eliezer, 80
Local determination, xxiv, 61, 66
Logic, 42-43
Loos, Adolph, 41
Luhmann, Niklas, 12, 46, 61-62, 63, 66
Lukács, György, ix, x, xvii
Lyotard, Jean-Francios, vii-xx

Mach, Ernst, 41
Malevitch, K. S., 78, 80
Mallarmé, Stéphane, xi
Mandel, Ernest, xiv
Mandelbrot, Benoit, 58
Marcuse, Herbert, 79
Marx, Karl, xix, xx, xxiv
Marxism, x, xiii-xv, 11, 12-13, 36-37
Master-narratives, xii, xix. *See also* Narrative
Mathematics, 42-43, 58-59
McIntyre, Alistair, xi
Medawar, P. B., ix, 60
Metalanguage, xxiii, 42, 43
Metanarrative, xxiv, xx, 34, 37
Mies Van Der Rohe, Ludwig, xvii
Mill, John Stuart, 42
Modernity: in art, 78; defined, xxiii; Haber-
mas on, xvii; vs. postmodernity, 79; and
realism, 77; theories of society in, 11-14
Montaigne, 81
Moore, Charles, xviii

"Moves." *See* Language games
Musil, Alois, 41

Napoleon. *See* Bonaparte
Narrative: decline of, xi, 15, 37-38, 41, 48-
49, 51, 60, 65; grand narrative of emancipation, xi, 31-32, 35-36, 39, 40, 48,
49, 60, 66; grand narrative of speculation, xi, 32-37, 38-39; and legitimation
of knowledge, 27-31; little, xi, 60;
validity of, 27. *See also* Knowledge
Nietzsche, Friedrich, xii, 39, 77, 81

Oliva, Achille Bonito, 73

Palo Alto school, 59
Paradox, xxv, 43, 54, 55, 60
Paradoxology, 4, 59
Paralogy, xix, 43, 60-61, 66
Parsons, Talcott, 11-12
Performance maximization. *See* Perform-
ativity
Performative: as linguistic notion, ix, x-xi;
statement, 9
Performativity: "advantages" of, 62-63; in
education, 47-53; and institutions, 17;
in Marxism, 12; in Parsons, 11; and post-
modernity, 41; in research, 44-47; in
scientific knowledge, 54-60, 64
Perrin, Jean, 56, 58
Petronius, Gaius, 79
Philosophy, crisis of, 41
Physics, 55, 56-58
Picasso, Pablo, 79, 80
Plato, 28-29
Popper, Karl, 72
"Postindustrial society," vii, xiii, xiv, 46-47
Post-Marxism, x
Postmodernism: defined, xxiv, 81; legitima-
tion in, 37, 41; and modernism, xvi-xvii,
xxiii, 79; and performance, 41; in
science, 53-60; and social bond, 11-14;
varieties of, xviii
Power: and knowledge, 5, 8, 36, 46, 47; and
legitimation, 47, 61, 62-63
Pragmatics: in aspects of language, 9-10; of
narrative knowledge, 18-23; of scientific
knowledge, 23-27, 28, 53, 64, 65; social
vs. scientific, 65
Prescriptive statements. *See* Language